Southern California
WEDDINGS

CAPTIVATING DESTINATIONS
AND EXCEPTIONAL RESOURCES
Introduced by the Finest Event Planners

Published by

PANACHE
P A N A C H E   P A R T N E R S

Panache Partners, LLC
1424 Cables Court
Plano, TX 75075
469.246.6060
Fax: 469.246.6062
www.panache.com

Publishers: Brian C. Carabet and John A. Shand

Printed in Malaysia

Distributed by Independent Publishers Group
800.888.4741

PUBLISHER'S DATA

Southern California Weddings

Library of Congress Control Number: 2011943193

ISBN 13: 978-1-933415-99-4
ISBN 10: 1-933415-99-1

First Printing 2012

10 9 8 7 6 5 4 3 2 1

Right: Melissa Musgrove Photography, page 230

Previous Page: John Russo Photography, page 49

Panache Partners, LLC, is dedicated to the restoration and
conservation of the environment. Our books are manufactured
with strict adherence to an environmental management system in
accordance with ISO 14001 standards, including the use of paper
from mills certified to derive their products from well-managed
forests. We are committed to continued investigation of alternative
paper products and environmentally responsible manufacturing
processes to ensure the preservation of our fragile planet.

Southern California
WEDDINGS

INTRODUCTION

Everything about a wedding should be a dream—the dress, the décor, the ceremony, and most definitely the location. While many couples find everything they could wish for in a venue close to home, for others the chance to combine wedding with vacation often proves irresistible. Enter the destination wedding.

And enter Southern California. Brimming with natural beauty, the sunny region makes it easy to find nuptial perfection. Chances are the weather will be just right on your special day, and thanks to a host of top-notch event professionals already in the area—well versed in catering to the most exacting stars—everything else will fall right into place. Romantic brides in search of beach ceremonies, chic brides aiming for Hollywood glam, and classic brides after elegant tradition are all drawn to the area's overflowing variety and style. Whatever the setting, Southern California truly has everything when it comes to weddings.

The pages to come will do nothing less than dazzle you. Ten chapters explore as many diverse destinations within Southern California, from the beaches of Santa Barbara to the desert oasis of Palm Springs to the sophistication and grandeur of Beverly Hills and Hollywood to the romantic charm of Santa Monica and San Diego—to name a few. Each chapter is authored by a leading event planner, who offers a personal introduction to the destination's magic, most interesting hotels and venues, and best in local catering, floral design, entertainment, photography, and other areas of specialty.

Southern California Weddings celebrates the Golden State's best wedding destinations and resources while acting as a priceless guide to making your dream day memorably perfect in every way. Eat, drink, and be married!

Jonathan Reeves
International Event Company
Leading the way in Beverly Hills, Jonathan Reeves joined the Four Seasons Los Angeles as director of catering in 1987, embarking on a career that defines elite entertaining. Eleven years and many soirées later, Jonathan joined the iconic Beverly Hills Hotel as catering and conference services director, and in 2000, he entered the world of private event planning. Today, he is principal of International Event Company, a premier event planning firm that specializes in destination weddings. While his creative team focuses primarily on weddings, they also have a reputation for producing exquisite social and corporate celebrations hosted in private homes and estates, country clubs, historic venues, beach settings, and renowned hotels.

Lisa Vorce
Oh, How Charming!
For signature celebrations and urban-chic weddings in Hollywood and downtown LA, Lisa Vorce has a vast repertoire of talent to call upon and a sensibility for the city. Cleaning ideas from the selected venue, its architecture and its energy, she and her specialists customize the day to reflect the bride and groom's specific taste and preferences. Whether a once-in-a-lifetime fête with a decidedly edgy vibe or with an elite private club ambience, the experience is certain to be flawless when Oh, How Charming! is in charge. Lisa knows what it takes: a general's strategy, a diplomat's negotiation, a concierge's direction, and a confidante's comfort.

Mindy Weiss
Mindy Weiss Party Consultants
Nobody knows Malibu like Mindy Weiss, and even though she plans weddings all over the country, she's partial to the seaside city for its beauty and air of exclusivity. Mindy ventured into the event world as an invitation designer, where she vowed to stay, but by popular demand she quickly transitioned into full-scale event planning. She is so passionate about orchestrating flawless events that she created her own iPhone app, giving brides everywhere access to her tried-and-true methods for staying organized. In addition to her primary role at Mindy Weiss Party Consultants, Mindy dabbles in an array of creative pursuits as writer, product designer, and lifestyle expert.

Jeannie Savage
Details Details
Drawing upon her extensive background in the luxury hospitality arena, Orange County expert Jeannie Savage knows her way around the best venues and locations for hosting incomparable weddings. She and her cadre of savvy, stylish event planners at Details Details are renowned for putting together fresh and exciting design concepts, creating a sensation throughout Southern California by specializing in celebrations for romantic destination weddings and multiple-day events. Her full-service approach translates to a passion for perfection, as is evident in every personalized detail, from selecting the most feminine bridal pumps to developing the most elegant reception theme.

Kristin Banta
Kristin Banta Events
With its classic architecture and an atmosphere of elegant simplicity, Palm Springs has long captured the hearts of movie stars and other style-savvy vacationers, which is why it's one of Kristin Banta's favorite wedding locales. Through her eponymous firm Kristin Banta Events, Kristin creates unforgettable celebrations while bringing a fresh perspective to the mix, always drawing on her invaluable background in fashion and entertainment. She is passionate about helping couples find their own voice for their wedding day, beginning each collaboration by uncovering what defines them as individuals, what makes them special together, and what they love.

Thomas Bui
Thomas Bui Lifestyle

Some of the finest weddings in San Diego are envisioned by Thomas Bui, who for more than a decade has been stunning brides, grooms, and all their guests with his distinctive designs that uniquely reflect the couple. Graced with a consuming passion and avant-garde sensibility, Thomas draws inspiration from haute couture to ensure that those in attendance leave with a beautiful lasting impression. Whether contemporary or chic, modern or glamorous, events designed by Thomas Bui Lifestyle truly showcase how the art of celebration has been perfected.

Colette and Kaitlin Lopez
La Fete

Deeply rooted in the culture and traditions of Santa Barbara, Colette and Kaitlin Lopez of La Fete know the city inside and out: the most talented people, beautiful venues, and interesting sites—on and off the beaten path. The mother-daughter entrepreneurs plan events of all scopes and styles, but they have developed quite a reputation for their breathtaking estate weddings. By handling each situation with calmness and grace, Colette and Kaitlin create stunning, stress-free environments. Always adding the perfect decorative accessories and collaborating closely with trusted local vendors, they develop alfresco spaces for dinner and dancing that feel warm and intimate yet fully embrace the natural majesty of their hometown.

Lisa Corjestani
Details Event Planning

A native Californian, Lisa Corjestani is convinced that seaside ceremonies are the way to go and recommends Santa Monica as one of the most scenic locales in the country, if not the world. Just as her firm's name, Details Event Planning, implies, Lisa's passion lies in the details, operating with the mantra that if it's important to the guests of honor, it's important to her. Because Lisa understands how overwhelming the process of planning a wedding can be, she makes a point of streamlining the bride and groom's involvement so that they can skip the headaches and experience all the fun and magic.

Rebecca Stone
Duet Weddings

Rebecca Stone's enthusiasm for and knowledge about Santa Ynez Valley simply bubbles over as soon as the subject arises. After planning her own wedding in the area, Rebecca fell in love with the wine country as well as with planning the big day. Duet Weddings was born and is the ultimate fulfillment of Rebecca's dream of indulging her natural tendencies and talents: love of food and wine, obsession with paper products, passion for flowers, interest in fashion, and an admittedly nerdy delight in color coding, list making, and labeling. What has made Rebecca a favorite of brides across the nation, though, is her infectious appreciation and celebration of love.

CONTENTS

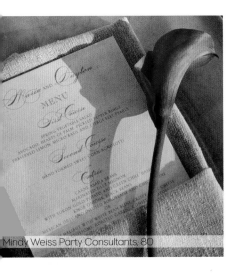

Mindy Weiss Party Consultants, 80

Isari Flower Studio + Event Design, 189

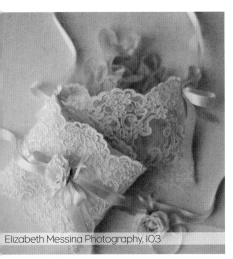

Elizabeth Messina Photography, 103

"*From the most posh of venues offering stellar service to custom catering, creative floral design, exquisite décor, and designer lighting, trusted resources are at your fingertips. You can keep things under the radar or let the paparazzi know you're here; it's entirely up to you.*" *Jonathan Reeves*

Beverly Hills

by Jonathan Reeves, International Event Company

Imagine shopping amongst celebrities along palm tree-lined Rodeo Drive, dining at five-star restaurants with award-winning chefs, pampering yourself at the most lavish salons and spas the world has to offer; welcome to a typical day in Beverly Hills, the city considered the mecca of luxury, glitz, and glamour. This is a city that truly has it all: haute couture, gourmet dining, arts and culture, and a movie star as your next-door neighbor. Home to many longtime residents from diverse cultures, Beverly Hills has a small-town feel while remaining the hub for international visitors. It's the only city in the world where even the zip code, 90210, is famous.

The mix of cultures makes the iconic city of 34,000 residents fascinating, offering a blend of European influences from luxury cars to renowned art galleries, famous hotels to high fashion. There is a mystique within this city; between movie moguls, over-the-top real estate, and acclaimed nightlife, you can't help but notice that Beverly Hills is where big ideas turn into overnight sensations.

Photographs: above ©iStockphoto.com/sister_lumiere; facing page ©iStockphoto.com/jmbatt

Located in the center of Los Angeles, Beverly Hills enjoys both sun-drenched days and Pacific marine breezes from nearby Santa Monica. The weather is perfect for lounging by the pool, picnicking at the historic Greystone Mansion, or shopping at The Golden Triangle—a must on any traveler's itinerary. As you stroll down Rodeo Drive, you'll recognize couture designers: Prada, Versace, Louis Vuitton, Dior, Cartier, and Tiffany & Company. Rodeo is a living theater of fashion, art, and people, impressive whether it's your first visit or one of many. People-watching is a visitor's pastime and celebrity sightings are an everyday phenomenon.

Photographs: above ©iStockphoto.com/LPETTET; top right Simone Van Kempen, Simone & Martin Photography; right by Nadine Froger Photography

14

Readily accessible from cities around the world via the Los Angeles International Airport, it's only a 20-minute scenic drive to Beverly Hills—a welcoming home base for your wedding party and guests as celebratory plans unfold naturally around its chic locale nestled between Bel Air and Hollywood. Indoor-outdoor weddings are a Beverly Hills tradition thanks to the desirable year-round weather. If you would like your ceremony in a formal garden, cocktails on a rooftop, or Sunday brunch on a lawn, anything is accomplishable. The most requested wedding dates are holiday weekends, particularly Memorial Day, the Fourth of July, and Labor Day, which allow guests to create an extended vacation. The holiday season is always popular as well, when the city comes to life with sparkling events and festive décor.

Beverly Hills is perfect for everyone, but especially for those with high expectations like entertainment industry clientele and savvy local residents. World-class service has become the Beverly Hills standard, making it a wonderful location for a dream wedding.

Photographs: above ©iStockphoto.com/ LPETTET; left by Nadine Froger Photography

Notably sophisticated and unique international weddings are a Beverly Hills specialty. It's a place where extravagant, multi-day celebrations can be orchestrated in grandiose fashion. We once planned a week-long wedding for an Indian bride and groom, part of which involved securing a live elephant for their culturally significant wedding procession known as the baraat. Escorted by his extended family, traditional drummers in formal costume, and festive Hindi music in the air, the groom gallantly rode down several city blocks on an adorned elephant into the porte-cochère of The Beverly Wilshire Hotel. Tai the elephant knelt down, gently delivering the groom to his wedding guests, while neighborhood residents, local media, and astonished tourists cheered. The elaborate parade culminated on the rooftop of the hotel for an exchange of flower garlands with the bride, followed by a ceremony and reception for 500 guests.

While perfect for such large family affairs, Beverly Hills is also ideal for intimate gatherings or high-profile celebrations. Its location in the heart of the entertainment industry means that some of the most sought-after performers—including legendary bands and DJs, "American Idol" singers, cirque acrobats, and Marilyn Monroe impersonators—are only a phone call away. From the most posh of venues offering stellar service to custom catering, creative floral design, exquisite décor, and designer lighting, trusted resources are at your fingertips. You can keep things under the radar or let the paparazzi know you're here; it's entirely up to you.

Photographs: above and facing page by Nadine Froger Photography; top right and right by Aaron Delesie

Just when you think you've seen it all, someone comes up with something new that reminds you this is a city where anything is possible. As your guests enjoy the weekend's festivities, they are treated to superb amenities that rival any on the planet, unique attractions to explore, and relaxing, five-star accommodations, making them feel like celebrities. With all-out glamour and excitement everywhere you turn, your Beverly Hills wedding will create memories that last a lifetime.

Photographs: above by Chris Ann Brunsmann, Chris Ann Photography; top left and left by Nadine Froger Photography; facing page by Yitzhak Dalal Photography

When it comes to hotels...

There is something for everyone within Beverly Hills' six square miles. Accommodations don't get any better than the Four Seasons Hotel Los Angeles at Beverly Hills, where the service is unparalleled and celebrity guests are the norm. With just one ballroom and a beautiful adjacent garden, your event is sure to be the hotel's only focus. There is also The Beverly Hills Hotel, better known as the "pink palace," where you can enjoy lunch at the famous Polo Lounge restaurant, or relax in a private cabana poolside. Known for hosting a myriad of events ranging from 400-person weddings to 20-person dinner parties, the hotel has a variety of ballrooms and gardens to choose from. If you would rather be in the center of it all, The Beverly Wilshire Hotel is a perfect option. As it's located at the base of Rodeo Drive, shopping, dining, and people watching are steps out the front door. Have cocktails in the famous penthouse suite, or host a dinner for 700 guests in the grand ballroom—the options are endless. Just down the street is the Montage Beverly Hills whose beautiful terrace is the perfect setting for a wedding ceremony. Looking for something different? Then the SLS Hotel at Beverly Hills is for you. Chic yet unconventional at the same time, it provides a completely novel guest experience.

Photographs courtesy of Four Seasons Hotel Los Angeles at Beverly Hills, top left by Nadine Froger Photography, event produced by Alyse Sobel Events & Consulting, left by David Michael Photography, below by Yitzhak Dalal Photography

Four Seasons Hotel Los Angeles at Beverly Hills

Inviting. Glamorous. Iconic.

On a quiet, palm-lined avenue near the heart of Beverly Hills lies the newly restyled ultra chic Four Seasons Hotel. Expansive terraces, balconies, and landscaped panoramas offer the ambience of a sunlit residence set in a lush garden. The setting alone has a romantic aura and the guestrooms promise an experience fit for royalty.

Photographs: above by John Solano Photography; top left by Nadine Froger Photography; left by Don Riddle

Choosing from the Presidential Suite or a supremely comfortable deluxe room with French doors, a room at Four Seasons begins with a liberating sense of space; your guestroom or suite is among the largest available in all of Los Angeles. Designed to inspire with contemporary furnishings and décor, its glamorous interior connects with the surrounding environment. Scenic views of the Hollywood Hills, Los Angeles, or Beverly Hills are right out your window so you know you have arrived. Close to trendsetting shopping and dining in the exclusive enclave of Beverly Hills, the legendary Four Seasons is where you'll want to be with family and friends.

Photographs: this page by Nadine Froger Photography; facing page by David Michael Photography

You'll enjoy a restful sleep because every sensory detail has been carefully refined, down to the precise depth of your marble soaking tub. Feeling thoroughly at home, and completely at your best, you're sure to be ready for the wedding celebration. Amenities abound at the Four Seasons, from the alfresco fitness center and pool to concierge services. Upon request, Four Seasons offers luxury Rolls Royce house car service complimentary for you and your visiting party to sightsee or gallery hop. The Italian restaurant Culina Modern Italian will awaken your taste buds with tantalizing modern cuisine and wine selections that may be enjoyed alfresco for a true Southern California dining experience. And sipping sophisticated cocktails at Windows Lounge, known as Hollywood's living room, will certainly inspire easy conversation. To wind down from a busy day, you may wish to indulge in a restful massage or rejuvenating treatment at the world-class spa. Welcoming the bride and groom, members of the bridal party, close relatives, or friends is a daily affair as the Four Seasons promises a luxurious and most memorable stay in LA.

Photographs: above by David Michael Photography; top right by Elizabeth Messina Photography; right by John Solano Photography; facing page top left by Jay Lawrence Goldman Photography; facing page top right by Yitzhak Dalal Photography; facing page bottom by John Solano Photography

When it comes to catering...

Delicious choices are everywhere, as Beverly Hills is known for its international flavors. The Kitchen for Exploring Foods will take you on an adventure in creative cuisine while providing five-star service. Guests have left events asking for recipes, especially for house specialties like the French toast casserole and warm chocolate bouchon cake. World-renowned Wolfgang Puck Catering, whose clientele include the Governors Ball at the Academy Awards®, is consistently creative and impressive. Savore Cuisine & Events is a great choice if you're looking for really unique flavors; its chefs are ever-inspired by the changing seasons and update their menus to reflect the freshest produce available. There is also An Catering, owned by the same family as the famous Crustacean restaurant, which is rooted in fresh and healthy cuisine. A unique, delicious, and decorative addition to any event can be found through Hasmik Party Services, which provides elaborate and abundant fruit displays, showcasing fresh, exotic, and colorful fruit beautifully arranged as a specialty buffet. The culinary experts serving Beverly Hills have a reputation for appealing to diverse palates, which is the kind of success that can only be achieved through years of experience.

Photographs: right courtesy of Wolfgang Puck Catering, by Ron Miller Photography; below left courtesy of The Kitchen for Exploring Foods, by Silvia Mautner Photography; below right courtesy of Savore Cuisine & Events, by Erez Levy

Savore Cuisine & Events
Sensational. Flawless. Delectable.

"There is no love sincerer than the love of food." Savore Cuisine's flavorful philosophy is based on an inspiring quote by Nobel Prize recipient George Bernard Shaw. The boutique catering and event firm serves an exclusive clientele throughout LA, creating the finest dining experiences imaginable.

Photographs by Erez Levy, Savore Cuisine & Events

Chef-owners Richard Lauter and Erez Levy, formerly of Spago Beverly Hills, develop constantly changing seasonal menus inspired by the highest quality ingredients available through their relationships with local farmers, artisans, and purveyors. Partner Michael Morrisette, former general manager of award-winning Melisse in Santa Monica, conducts Savore's beautiful and professional wait staff with the precision and grace of a ballet. His production skills and service philosophy allow the Savore team a masterful control over the event environment and the overall guest experience.

Photographs by Erez Levy, Savore Cuisine & Events

With a passion for cutting-edge culinary theory, Savore creates a product that is artful and stylish, but always focused on flavor. Its menus often express modern interpretations of global comfort foods, inspired by the culinary visions and histories of its clientele. Savore has taken wedding catering to new heights of personalization—a comprehensive process of methodical menu and service planning, bride and groom interviews, and menu tastings that feel more like sophisticated dinner parties.

Savore specializes in redefining the social dining experience. Events range from tray-passed small plates grazing menus to family-style buffets served on each guest-seating table, and from seated multi-course tasting menus to a progression of performance tapas stations. Whatever the direction or event theme, a fresh innovative menu presented artfully and served professionally is the Savore trademark.

Photographs by Erez Levy, Savore Cuisine & Events

29

An Catering
Tradition. Healthy. Divine.

Since becoming a landmark in Southern California, Crustacean Beverly Hills has spawned a successful catering division, An Catering, which was founded by executive chef Helene "Mama" An and her daughter Catherine. Their delicious "secret kitchen" makes appearances at offsite weddings, private events, and more. Dubbed as "star caterer to the stars" by the *Los Angeles Times*, An Catering has become a household name in the social circles of Beverly Hills and at Hollywood events. The family company focuses on transforming fresh and organic ingredients into divinely inspired dishes that keep guests buzzing about the menu long after the celebration.

Photographs: above by Jessica Boone; top and bottom left by Alex Vasilescu

The Kitchen for Exploring Foods
Taste. Presentation. Temptation.

Southern California has a tantalizing secret that locals are privy to: The Kitchen for Exploring Foods. Winning the taste buds of savvy partygoers, Peggy Dark is at the top of the class when it comes to preparing fabulous fare, creating sophisticated cuisine that rivals gourmet restaurants anywhere. Her catering prowess is revered, and the star-studded town of Beverly Hills is her preferred place to create mouthwatering multi-course presentations, earning the catering company the Zagat award of distinction. Wedding receptions that rely on Peggy's flair for food can expect innovative dishes that delight the senses. Guests love to savor her fresh creations, often subtle, sometimes spicy, always refined—a true gastronomic adventure.

Photographs: right by Silvia Mautner Photography; below and bottom right by Joy Marie Photography

Wolfgang Puck Catering
Passionate. Inspired. Welcoming.

"Live, love, eat!" is the mantra of renowned chef Wolfgang Puck. Your wedding day embodies the same qualities: sharing food, expressing love, and celebrating to the fullest. Committed to using the freshest natural ingredients, grown and prepared with care, Wolfgang Puck Catering is part innovation, part tradition, combining fabulous food with stellar service and attention to detail. Its talented chefs can satisfy any palate, whether the desire is for global flavors, delicious meals that meet dietary considerations, or a family favorite. Wolfgang's fine dining roots inspire his team's restaurant-quality approach with skillful preparation, personalized service, and countless options, so your delicious feast fits you perfectly, just like your gown.

Photographs: top courtesy of Wolfgang Puck Catering; above by Person + Killian Photography; right by Aihara Visuals Photography

When it comes to floral design...

Stylistic options range from classic to dramatic, and everything in between. Creativity defines Mark's Garden, whose innovative style and imagination make your event truly unique while still delivering an incredible value for your investment. Empty Vase has a reputation for creating beautiful and unexpected, large-scale statements such as an enormous Jewish ceremony huppah set up in the middle of the ballroom, covered in thousands of red roses. There is also The Hidden Garden, known for designing a very romantic feel, which carries through from the ceremony to the reception and even the honeymoon suite. LA Premier has perfected the art of floral production and transforms each event into a vital component of visual design excellence. Getting married in Beverly Hills means love is in bloom—big time!

Photographs: above courtesy of LA Premier, by Joshua Bobrove; top left courtesy of The Hidden Garden, by A. Niesing; left courtesy of Empty Vase

33

Empty Vase
Beauty. Artful. Couture.

With a long list of celebrity clientele, Empty Vase creates posh and imaginative flower arrangements for the style-conscious crowd. In addition to lavish contemporary designs, flower aficionados can indulge in the beauty of exquisite floral arrangements and hard-to-find seasonal plants. Everyday, rose, and couture collections make the shop well-suited for high-end Beverly Hills weddings and parties.

Photograph courtesy of Empty Vase

Owner Saeed Babaeean and his team are careful to ensure that each element is crafted to harmonize with the theme and mood of the occasion—whether they're acting exclusively as floral designers or whether they've taken on the role of full-scale event designers. They can glean inspiration from anywhere: the bridal gown, a favorite color, or another element with personal meaning. The Empty Vase professionals' ability to connect with event hosts on a personal level—so that they feel entirely comfortable divulging their wildest floral dreams and desires—gives them a decided advantage in creating wholly personalized designs that enhance and define the event.

Photograph courtesy of Empty Vase

The Hidden Garden
Artistic. Inspiring. Perfect.

Inspired by the unique nature of each nuptial ceremony and reception, The Hidden Garden has the golden touch at marrying emotions and flowers. Traditional beauty, lush gardens, chic sophistication, rich romance, and vibrant love are just a few creative approaches from the shop's array of floral genres. Their unconventional style features a skillful display of color coupled with organic textures and the highest quality products, which has become the shop's hallmark.

Photographs: left by John Solano Photography; below left and right by David Michael Photography

The Hidden Garden's talented team creates detailed bouquets, intricate table centerpieces, abundant focal points, and lush ceremony settings to adorn the venue and complement the wedding party. Globally sourced flowers are hand-picked based on their petal quality, vibrant hues, and distinguishing features. Artful designs may stem from the bride's idea, a monochromatic color theme, to a whimsical garden fantasy, making every floral accent a personalized statement. Knowing that a bride's wedding vision is as individual as she is, The Hidden Garden promises to fulfill the dream perfectly.

Photographs: above by John Solano Photography; top right and right by Couture Foto

LA Premier
Magic. Explore. Cherish.

Passion and detailed expertise give way to innovative and stylish events. Creators of magic inspired by all things fabulous, LA Premier is a special events design firm extraordinaire with a talented team led by founder Kevin Lee. The designers have the sensibility and inspirational eye to make all of their creations unique, fresh, and trend setting. From lavish flowers and lush colors to subtle accents, each event has an image all its own.

Photographs courtesy of LA Premier

Imagine partnering with your wedding designer to dream up a fantasy wedding with stately, stylish ceremonies and fairytale floral. Enjoy your special day and share the treasured moments of elegance and artistry with your guests. Everything comes to life as you celebrate in style surrounded by glamour and beauty, creating memories to cherish always.

Photographs courtesy of LA Premier

Mark's Garden
Signature. Inspiring. Breathtaking.

Dubbed "The Celebrity Florist" by the media, Mark Held of Mark's Garden is an extraordinary artist who uses flowers as his medium. From impressive weddings to the annual Academy Awards® Governors Ball and high-profile galas, glamorous events are his forte. Mark is an imaginative and knowledgeable designer who has set the standard for florists throughout Southern California since establishing his own studio and business. He personally selects the flowers that his team of designers uses on a daily basis and continually introduces new floral species, design styles, and color combinations to the local scene.

Photographs by Nadine Froger Photography

When it comes to cakes and invitations...

Joanie & Leigh's Cake Divas is exceptional at creating a custom recipe that is personally significant to you, with a design that will make a statement in the room. Combining fresh-baked flavors and flawless icing in artistic form is a Beverly Hills tradition at Rosebud Cakes, whose pastry chef believes the design of your cake is paramount, whether it is intended to match the color scheme, display the bride and groom's unique personalities, or simply tie into the décor. Before indulging in sweets, mark your event with a printed promise of the festivities ahead in a well-designed invitation from Marc Friedland Couture Communications. Oscar® winners' envelope designer and branding guru Marc's communications tease with anticipation, whether your wedding is formal or playful. For high-profile and celebrity clientele, Lehr & Black Invitationers designs invitations ranging from colorful feathers and rhinestone-studded velvet to pop-up books; the designers' distinctive creations are guaranteed to shock your guests and leave them anxious to see what you have planned for them. The talented graphic designers of Bovary & Butterfly have an eye for craftsmanship and attention to detail that results in invitations and event branding that really expresses the hosts' style and presents a story for the receiver to unravel. Cakes and invitations created in Beverly Hills are crème de la crème, delicious, and enticing on every level.

Photographs: above courtesy of Marc Friedland Couture Communications, by John Ellis; right courtesy of Joanie & Leigh's Cake Divas

Joanie & Leigh's Cake Divas
Delicious. Elegant. Creative.

Over the top, elegant, fun, or out of this world, Cake Divas has been serving up specialty cakes with style in the Beverly Hills and LA area for years. Designs start with hand-drawn sketches, then cakes are made from scratch in the bakery and executed to perfection. Leigh Crode and Joan Spitler, or "the girls" as Hollywood's A-list affectionately calls them, are the masterminds behind Cake Divas. Together they share a passion for creating scrumptious and gorgeous wedding cakes, whether elegant, whimsical, lavish, or simply sublime.

Photographs by Leigh Crode

Traditional tiered wedding reception cakes, grooms cakes, or luscious rehearsal dinner cupcakes are whipped up and decorated to order, fulfilling every bridal couple's dream. Anything is possible and the ladies of Cake Divas have certainly proven their creativity by making towering tiers of fondant-covered rounds and flawlessly frosted buttercream squares with imaginative innovation. From handcrafted gum paste flowers and icing figures to sugar art details, painting and custom flavors, they do it all. "If you can dream it, we can create it!" is the duo's motto, and wedding couples agree that a confectionary creation from Cake Divas brings irresistible taste and beauty to the single most important celebration of their lives.

Photographs by Leigh Crode

Marc Friedland Couture Communications

Tactile. Dimensional. Original.

The art of the invitation thrives in the bustling LA atelier of Marc Friedland Couture Communications and its experiential design agency, Creative Intelligence, Inc., as it has for 25 years and counting. Known as the remarkable maven of the most beautiful and coveted invitations and event branding, Marc designs and produces stationery and invitations that transform luxurious papers, materials, and printing processes into magical, memorable works of art that you and your guests will always treasure. From the first-ever iconic Academy Awards® envelope to spectacular designs for corporate galas, Marc's genius concepts, color palettes, and tasteful approaches are sought by savvy event designers and party hosts around the world.

Photographs by John Ellis

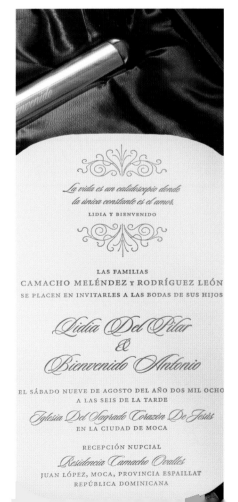

*La vida es un caleidoscopio donde
la única constante es el amor.*
LIDIA Y BIENVENIDO

LAS FAMILIAS
CAMACHO MELÉNDEZ Y RODRÍGUEZ LEÓN
SE PLACEN EN INVITARLES A LAS BODAS DE SUS HIJOS

*Lidia Del Pilar
&
Bienvenido Antonio*

EL SÁBADO NUEVE DE AGOSTO DEL AÑO DOS MIL OCHO
A LAS SEIS DE LA TARDE
Iglesia Del Sagrado Corazón De Jesús
EN LA CIUDAD DE MOCA

RECEPCIÓN NUPCIAL
Residencia Camacho Ovalles
JUAN LÓPEZ, MOCA, PROVINCIA ESPAILLAT
REPÚBLICA DOMINICANA

Combining impeccable style and meticulous craftsmanship, Marc and his team of designers and artisans create materials that are as unique as your romance. From modern and elegant to classic and chic, each stationery ensemble is a one-of-a-kind masterpiece that fills your journey to nuptial nirvana with unlimited joy and individuality. Author of the best-selling book *Invitations by Marc Friedland*, Marc has received many accolades for his fresh thinking and flawless execution. Both eye-catching and emotionally stirring, original dimensional designs highlight his beautiful wedding repertoire. Unlike standard invitations, Marc's work lives up to his company's name in that everything his team creates is bespoke and couture.

Photographs by John Ellis

When it comes to preserving memories...

Beverly Hills has a fleet of talented photographers who are experts in telling the story of a wedding day. Soulful, formal, artistic, candid, staged, or arranged—the choice is yours. Yitzhak Dalal can "paint" your timeless portrait like a family heirloom while John Solano catches the more relaxed reactions and often hidden moments of the day. Jay Lawrence Coldman has a remarkable edge to his gallery-quality photojournalistic work. With the intuition and perspective of an artist, John Russo's noteworthy experience with celebrities brings star power to your celebration. With a sensitive approach of sensuous and dreamlike images, the international fine art masters of Simone & Martin put you in your best light.

Photographs: right by Jay Lawrence Coldman Photography; below by John Solano Photography; bottom right courtesy of Nobu Los Angeles-West Hollywood

Jay Lawrence Goldman Photography
People. Sunshine. Original.

When Jay Goldman wants to really get his creativity flowing, he will start his day in the studio by stylizing a ring with clever lighting techniques or unexpected objects—a lollipop or a high heel, for instance—to create a real work of art. His approach to shooting bridal portraits and weddings is equally innovative, but of course the people take center stage. He has a stealthy way of being in the right place at the right moment, which is a skill that only comes with careful observation, innate talent, and years of experience.

Photographs by Jay Lawrence Goldman Photography

John Russo Photography
Celebrity. Lifestyle. Honest.

Celebrity photographer John Russo has made quite a name for himself in Beverly Hills. His work captures the pure essence of individuals. Whether he's shooting the hottest film stars, lifestyle editorials, or the world's top fashion magazine covers, his creative approach is undeniably honest. John's work has been featured on over 300 covers, making him one of the most sought-after celebrity photographers. His trained eye and technical acuity always reveals the true person. If you're fortunate enough to book this renowned talent for your wedding, his ability to capture emotional authenticity and spontaneity is simply amazing.

Photographs by John Russo Photography

John Solano Photography
Extraordinary. Vision. Passion.

Unbridled creativity is a rarity in any profession. John Solano has been photographing wedding couples with a passion, preserving life's special times through skillful use of his lens. Like a sports photographer, he looks for unpredictable reactions during the highlights of an event and also focuses on the more relaxed, candid moments. He fell in love with photography at 16, and today, with decades of experience, he is known for his unique perspective, high energy, and unobtrusive approach. John's photographs illuminate the romance, personalities, and festivities of the day with an unexpected twist on the traditional.

Photographs by John Solano Photography

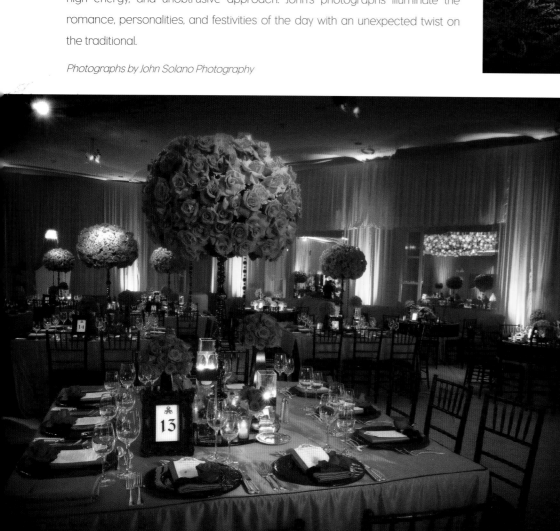

Yitzhak Dalal Photography
Masterful. Cinematic. Expressive.

Embodying the art of photography, Yitzhak Dalal has an intense passion for his life's work. Yitzhak uses his highly developed intuition and imagination, capturing images that reveal the beauty of emotions expressed as the wedding day unfolds. His success is founded on a soulful quality within each photograph, an intangible essence that you just can't put into words. He sees beyond the composition, capturing natural moments shared by the happy couple and guests. The end result is a series of photographs depicting the romance, ceremony, and celebration—an artful collection of heartfelt images for the bride and groom to treasure.

Photographs by Yitzhak Dalal Photography

Kasha Ensemble
Talented. Energetic. International.

Choosing the right wedding band can be a daunting decision. Finding professional musicians and vocalists with a repertoire of popular songs and international music ideal for dancing is even harder. Led by founding director Allen C. Nazarian, Kasha Ensemble offers a variety of international music performed by an inspiring multilingual group that can sing Top 40 hits in six languages. The world band's talent for delighting wedding guests is proven, especially when backed by the showmanship of its 16-piece orchestra.

Photographs: above by Behzad Photography; top left by Nejati Studios; left by John Solano Photography

The musicians' brand of electrifying energy and precision makes them perfect for private functions in sophisticated venues and concert halls. The Kasha Ensemble will dress in black-tie attire, all white wardrobes, or a more casual style to suit the desired formality. Because the quality of entertainment determines the happiness of guests, Kasha Ensemble ensures that every event is filled with great sounds and rhythms and thrilled audiences.

Photographs: right by John Solano Photography; below by Robert David

Nobu Los Angeles-West Hollywood
Acclaimed. Fresh. Global.

An unparalleled sushi experience awaits you at award-winning NOBU Los Angeles-West Hollywood. Opened in the spring of 2008, designed by world-renowned architect David Rockwell in the famed L'Orangerie space on La Cienega Boulevard, the restaurant has become synonymous with fresh and original sushi artistry invented by Chef Nobu Matsuhisa, served in a contemporary atmosphere of Japanese-inspired elegance.

Photographs: left and bottom left by Michael Bulbenko; below by Edmond Ho

NOBU has three separate dining rooms and an elegant bar and lounge. Each of the three spaces—the main dining room with sushi bar, the terrace, and the atrium—has its own unique character and feel. Whether attending an intimate seated dinner for 20 or a cocktail party for 300, guests will enjoy NOBU's innovative fare and exceptional service. The bar and lounge have become a Hollywood hotspot offering a tempting tapas menu designed for a more relaxed dining experience. In addition to signature dishes, there are local specials like wagyu tacos, Chilean seabass jalapeño miso, and kanpachi sashimi with baby artichoke and yuzu dressing. NOBU Los Angeles-West Hollywood has full catering services available for any affair.

Photographs: above by Clark Takahashi; right by Edmond Ho

NOBU Los Angeles-West Hollywood is a remarkable venue for customized events of sophistication with an accent on exotic taste. In 1994, Chef Nobu opened his original namesake restaurant in New York City; it was an instant success and became a magnet for food lovers and celebrities alike. Today, NOBU restaurants are a worldwide phenomenon with more than 20 locations around the globe.

Photographs: above by Edmond Ho; left and top left by Michael Bulbenko

Resource One Inc.
Textures. Patterns. Refined.

Roberta Karsch is the creative designer and founder of Resource One Inc., a boutique design firm serving the Beverly Hills community for over 20 years. Her passion is creating customized luxury linens and decorative accessories. Resource One Inc. was the first to introduce the original Philippe Starck ghost chairs for Beverly Hills weddings. The firm offers an array of exquisite linens and accessories that will make your dream wedding a reality. You'll choose from an expansive collection of table linens, napkins, runners, and unique chair treatments. Custom colors and sumptuous fabrics are emphasized, including embroidered organzas, embossed velvets, pure silks, sequins, rosettes, and many more.

Photographs by Duke Photography

Downtown LA
by Lisa Vorce, Oh, How Charming!

My enthusiasm for Hollywood and downtown LA may seem cliché, but here it goes: "Hooray for Hollywood," the title from the classic 1937 song, now the theme melody of the Academy Awards®. I believe that nothing conjures up more glamorous images in your mind than Old Hollywood and the internationally famous hills with the iconic sign. And who doesn't love cruising in a convertible all around LA? I am passionate about planning weddings in Los Angeles, and savvy brides love the locale, too.

Urbanites unite! Weddings in Hollywood and downtown LA are city-slicker chic, held in the midst of the bustling metropolis with its constant buzz and deeply rooted, culturally rich California lifestyle. There are great contemporary venues for hosting wedding ceremonies, receptions, and any of your pre- and post-parties from rehearsal dinners to late-night dance lounges. Couples can choose from so many hip and beautiful locations, including the Walt Disney Concert Hall, The London West Hollywood, Mondrian Los Angeles, The Smog Shoppe, a green urban oasis, or an exclusive social club such as The Jonathan Club, the glam Ebell Club, or the legendary California Club for the traditionalist.

Photographs: above ©iStockphoto.com/oversnap; facing page ©iStockphoto.com/ekash

For one bride, we designed a reception at the Sunset Tower Hotel as a truly elegant Hollywood affair. The famous landmark building, with its original Art Deco flair and star-studded history, was the perfect venue choice for a formal wedding. But having your wedding in the city is not for the faint of heart. It takes a bit more logistical planning to get you to the church or venue on time, thanks to crazy LA traffic. Weather is usually sunny year-round, but you can't rule out the chilly June gloom or an unexpected shower that may occur. A backup plan is always a must, especially if you are having an outdoor reception.

Photographs by Elizabeth Messina Photography

Before the big day, be sure to work in some sightseeing opportunities for yourself, your bridal party, and out-of-town guests because there's so much to do in LA. And the dining scene is a foodie's paradise. Imagine treating your guests to an après theatre evening of sushi at Katsuya across from the Pantages Theatre where you can catch a great Broadway show. For a really unique experience, check out the highly rated Bottega Louie or romantic Cicada for an Italian meal, or listen to live jazz and dine at The Edison restaurant, set in LA's first power plant and full of industrial ambience. Or head to Sixth Street and sip cocktails at the Rooftop Bar in The Standard Downtown LA for a bird's-eye view of the skyline at night. And for an afternoon of serious shopping, you can't

beat the Melrose Avenue boutiques interspersed with great eateries. Then there's Olvera Street, several city blocks featuring charming outdoor cafés and a colorful authentic Spanish vibe replete with street mariachis, providing an ideal rehearsal dinner site with its festive traditional Mexican fare and marketplace atmosphere. Throughout Hollywood and downtown LA, ethnic restaurants abound and are tucked away in their respective neighborhoods. There's Chinatown and Little Tokyo with tempting tastes plus exotic Argentinian and Cuban specialties sprinkled in for good measure. Trust me, the most well-traveled and sophisticated guests will not be disappointed with the global culture that LA has to offer.

Photographs by Elizabeth Messina Photography

LA means nonstop action. Grauman's Chinese Theatre is a classic haunt for movie buffs and strolling along the Hollywood Walk of Fame is always a crowd pleaser. How about taking your wedding party to MOCA for a guided tour of its vast contemporary art collection? Then there's the renowned Hollywood Bowl and The Orpheum Theatre for concerts and film, and the ultra cool and edgy Nokia Theatre entertainment campus. Catch some sports highlights at the Staples Center before the wedding day, where the Lakers, Clippers, and LA Kings play. Bowling at Lucky Strike just may be the unconventional bonding experience your wedding party would enjoy, or try an evening at The Greek Theatre for some great music to relax and unwind before the hectic day. And remember, sneaking in spa treatments at your hotel is a welcome respite to any busy pre-wedding schedule.

Photographs by Cheri Pearl

LA has evolved into a modern and trendsetting area with lots of soul and has been newly improved, but it is still very much in touch with its traditional California roots. Getting here is easy. You and your wedding guests simply fly into LAX, book your favorite city-based boutique hotel, and either rent a car or cab it conveniently around town. LA is still "where it's at" and the perfect place for a modern wedding large or small, whether you want it elegant, glitzy, über chic, or anything in between.

Photographs by Laura Kleinhenz, Docuvitae

When it comes to hotels...

The Ritz-Carlton, Los Angeles is a classic choice with all of the luxurious amenities, exquisite décor, fine dining, and breathtaking views you'd expect with the international name. If you're looking for a little bit of history, tour Sunset Tower Hotel, which is billed as the place where Old Hollywood becomes new, and was once home to the likes of Marilyn Monroe, Elizabeth Taylor, and Frank Sinatra. The London West Hollywood has an altogether different vibe as its décor marries the best of cosmopolitan chic and California cool. If you want to totally escape the hustle of the city and feel like you're in a foreign land, Figueroa Hotel is the place to be; its common spaces and boutique Moroccan rooms and suites are fabulously authentic.

Photographs: above courtesy of The London West Hollywood, by Paul Von Rieter; top left courtesy of The Ritz-Carlton, Los Angeles, by Kathleen Price; left courtesy of The London West Hollywood

The London West Hollywood
Legendary. Brilliant. Renowned.

Iconic Hollywood glamour mixes with modern sophistication and intuitive service at The London West Hollywood. Perched in the Hollywood Hills just steps from the legendary Sunset Strip and Beverly Hills, the hotel embodies the vision of a bold team of international tastemakers, presenting the perfect backdrop for impeccably staged events. Interiors designed by the renowned David Collins Studio and dining by heralded Chef Gordon Ramsay are all enhanced by service that is knowledgeable, friendly, and unobtrusive.

Photographs by Paul Von Rieter

A fusion of both its namesake cities, The London West Hollywood emulates the best of cosmopolitan chic and California cool. Exchange vows against an unforgettable background of flowering gardens and breathtaking views. Dance the night away in an elegant ballroom or atop the hotel's signature rooftop terrace overlooking the Hollywood Hills. Toast with friends within a stylish private dining salon or spacious suite. Timeless style, award-winning food and drink, and exquisite event space awaits.

Photographs: top courtesy of The London West Hollywood; above and right by Paul Von Rieter

The hotel is known for outdoor event spaces with stunning views of the city skylines and Hollywood Hills. The Hampton Court, bordered by white roses and box hedges, looks out to downtown Los Angeles, while the rooftop terrace and pool deck offer panoramic vistas and amazing sunset moments.

All cuisine, from appetizers to desserts, is conceived and prepared by the Gordon Ramsay team under the direction of executive chef Anthony Keene, who creates menus infused with local artisan flavors and California's abundance of fresh produce and seafood. This level of innovative gourmet within a boutique Los Angeles hotel is wholly unique to The London West Hollywood. In addition, The London's breakfast table—a buffet-style bounty of sweet and savory morning bites along with specialty coffees—is complimentary to all hotel guests.

Photographs by Paul Von Rieter

The Ritz-Carlton, Los Angeles
Luxury. Sophistication. Sleek.

A sumptuous urban oasis, The Ritz-Carlton, Los Angeles is positioned at the heart of exciting downtown Los Angeles. Located just steps from Walt Disney Concert Hall, The Museum of Contemporary Art, and the Nokia Theatre LA Live, the hotel offers close proximity to countless dynamic cultural opportunities while remaining an intimate respite from the hustle and bustle of the outside world. An abundance of stunningly well-appointed guestrooms and WP24, the award-winning restaurant and lounge from celebrity chef Wolfgang Puck, await those who desire a truly magnificent experience.

Photographs: above by Kathleen Price; top right by Ryan Cobuty, Gensler; right by Jerry Atnip

When it comes to venues...

I love Vibiana, which has been thoughtfully transformed from a 19th-century cathedral into a haven for exquisite events. A 1920s gem, Cicada is a beautiful restaurant that embodies the glamour of the Art Deco era with a contemporary twist. Another space that I'm attracted to for its aesthetic as well as its history is Marvimon, which was originally built as an automobile showroom and has a fabulous open floorplan and soaring ceilings.

Photographs courtesy of Vibiana: right by Next Exit Photography; below by Evoke Photography; below right courtesy of Vibiana

When it comes to catering...

One of my favorite resources is The Food Matters; chef Jerry Baker certainly has his priorities straight, basing all of his culinary creations on principles of quality ingredients, fresh flavors, and impeccable presentation. New West Catering is owned by Jeff and Janet Olsson, who believe in preparing everything by hand using as many local ingredients as possible. Patina Restaurant Group is the realized vision of restaurateur Nick Valenti and master chef Joachim Splichal, whose catering services grew organically from their restaurant patrons' requests, which shows just how tasty their fare is. And of course you can't go wrong with the signature cuisine of Trés LA, which always makes an impression with guests.

Photographs courtesy of Wolfgang Puck Catering

When it comes to floral design...

It's always impressive to see what Mindy Rice Floral Design can do, whether the occasion calls for rustic elegance, authentic Indian, or another niche genre. R. Jack Balthazar really knows how to make the process fun, and because it's owned by a husband and wife team that also does event design, you get the benefit of really broad perspectives. The floral designers at Empty Vase are insanely talented and never cease to amaze, always inventing truly unique creations regardless of how traditional or contemporary the request. Mille Fiori Floral Design is another solid resource that has been a major contributor to the high-end events scene for many years and even offers floral workshops so that everyone from novice to pro can benefit from the team's expert tips and tricks.

Photographs: above courtesy of R. Jack Balthazar, by Yvette Roman Photography; right courtesy of Mille Fiori Floral Design, by 2me Studios

Mille Fiori Floral Design
Accents. Unexpected. Vibrant.

When taken literally, Mille Fiori means one thousand flowers. But over the years that Gina Park and her team of extraordinarily talented designers have been in love with flowers, they've found that nothing about them can be taken literally. Stepping into their rose-scented world is like entering an extremely lovely, textural, and fragrant dream, a feeling they replicate time and again with each wedding they work on.

Photographs by Sean Twaney, 2me Studios; left design by Iconic Event Studios

It's always a plus when people on the event design team have really diverse backgrounds and can lend insight and expertise in areas beyond their current focus. With the exquisite floral arrangements of R. Jack Balthazar, that's exactly what owners Rene and Niki Delacueva have to offer. Their event design experience certainly plays into all of their floral offerings, which are developed to fit cohesively into the overall vision while standing on their own as true works of art.

Photographs by Niki Delacueva

R. Jack Balthazar's portfolio of fabulous events and floral styles is insanely diverse, spanning romantic Moroccan motifs, retro-chic sensibilities, and organic wine country opulence, among other distinct looks. Never content to simply design beautiful centerpieces or accent arrangements, the team seeks to evoke distinct emotions and ambiences of cherished cultures, places, and memories through their brand of bespoke floral design.

Photographs: left by Jose Mandojana, Docuvitae; bottom left by Niki Delacueva; below by Elizabeth Messina Photography

THE FAVOUR OF YOUR REPLY
IS REQUESTED BY THE FIRST OF JUNE

ℛℛ.ℬ.ℙ.

𝓜

ACCEPTS WITH PLEASURE

DECLINES WITH REGRET

MEAT

FISH

VEGETARIAN

Thank You

199 NEW MONTGOMERY STREET
UNIT 1510
SAN FRANCISCO, CALIFORNIA 94105

MR. AND MRS. FRANK YU
REQUEST THE PLEASURE OF YOUR COMPANY
AT THE MARRIAGE OF THEIR DAUGHTER

Helen S. Yu

TO

Dr. Michael M. Kuo

SON OF
MR. AND MRS. SHU PENG KUO
ON SATURDAY, THE FOURTH OF JULY
TWO THOUSAND AND NINE
AT FIVE THIRTY IN THE AFTERNOON

THE RITZ-CARLTON, LAGUNA NIGUEL
DANA POINT, CALIFORNIA

RECEPTION TO FOLLOW

FORMAL ATTIRE

When it comes to cakes and invitations...

Sweet and Saucy Shop is an absolute winner, known for gourmet cakes, cupcakes, cookies, and other homemade delicacies—the pastry chefs even offer baking and decorating classes. A bakery of a different flavor, Sweet Lady Jane focuses on really unique cake flavors like blackout espresso fudge, hazelnut mousse, and chocolate candied orange, all of which are almost too pretty to eat. Like many fine stationers, Sugar Paper embraces the timeless tradition of letterpress, which dates back to the 15th century; it's so beautiful that recipients can sense the quality even without knowing the history. Papel Paper & Press offers fabulously boutique invitations and other printed pieces, all customized to convey just the right message for the occasion. Tiny Pine Press has made quite a name for itself in terms of sustainable designs that incorporate recycled paper and soy ink, though more traditional materials and techniques are certainly available as necessary to achieve the desired look.

Photographs: above left and right courtesy of Wolfgang Puck Catering; left courtesy of Laura Hooper Calligraphy, by Steve Steinhardt Photography

77

When it comes to preserving memories...

Do your research before you meet with photographers and videographers so that you already have an idea of the styles you like. It's easy to get swept away by someone's portfolio, and even if the professional is undeniably talented, you want to make sure that you know your options. Aaron Delesie is someone I've worked with for many years, and I love the way he captures authentic moments with such ease. Though she can shoot in an array of styles, Elizabeth Messina has a very romantic way of looking at the world, which allows her to truly translate people's emotions into the two-dimensional medium. Jose Villa takes more of an editorial approach to his still photography, offering unexpected compositions that eloquently convey the mood of the moment. Curtis Heyne with Living Cinema knows the value of capturing those moments through a medium that is simply uninterrupted. And another favorite of mine is Paper Tape Films; with local filmmakers and a production team that has impressive Hollywood experience, the results are always unbelievable.

Photographs by Aaron Delesie

Photograph by Elizabeth Messina Photography

Malibu
by Mindy Weiss, Mindy Weiss Party Consultants

The city of Malibu has always been cloaked in an air of mystery and glamour. What began as a private hideaway for a millionaire businessman and his wife has since blossomed into an area famous for its robust mountains, wooded canyons, and, of course, its 20 miles of glistening coastline. The exclusivity that Malibu was built on has extended into present day, as it's still the home to a veritable list of who's who in the entertainment and business worlds. But the gated mansions, hidden behind lush palm trees and trailing bougainvillea, only add to the tingling sense of excitement. You're where the celebrities—since 1928, when Cary Cooper, Gloria Swanson, Barbara Stanwyck, and others turned the area into the "Malibu Movie Colony"—have come to live and play.

Though it was only incorporated into a city in 1991, Malibu's history goes back much further. When Frederick Hastings Rindge purchased the land known as "Rancho Malibu" from the Spanish in 1892, the future founder of Pacific Life and his wife, Rhoda May, guarded their new home with zeal. Rhoda May even took advantage of a little-known law and built a small railroad on their property to prevent Southern Pacific Railroad from laying tracks through and spoiling their paradise. In 1929, however, the state won a larger battle when it

Photographs: above ©iStockphoto.com/LoveToShoot; facing page ©iStockphoto.com/pastorscott

gained permission to build what is now one of the most well-known and picturesque roads in America: the Pacific Coast Highway. With the highway, Malibu was suddenly opened up to the rest of the country, and hundreds flocked to the area that Frederick had once said rivaled the showplaces of Italy and France.

But what Malibu is truly known for is its beaches. To be married on the same beaches where Gidget, Annette Funicello, and Frankie Avalon did the twist is a nostalgic incentive for some, while others are drawn to the namesake city of Malibu Barbie for its abundance of sunshine and surf. Zuma Beach, Point Dume State Beach, Surfrider Beach, Westward Beach—the

Photographs: above by John Solano Photography; top left by Simone & Martin Photography, simonemartin.com; left ©iStockphoto.com/LoveToShoot

crashing waves and glittering sand can relax even the most stressed-out brides. Although the beach may seem like a carefree spot for a ceremony, Malibu is actually very strict with its permits and doesn't allow any events on the sand unless you have legal access to one of the nearby beachfront properties. Fortunately these gorgeous homes can be rented for the occasion, although it would be wise to make sure the space is adequate and that all other necessary permits have been obtained. I think that having your ceremony in a private home lends an extra-special touch to a wedding; very few other couples will share that spot. It's important to be mindful of Malibu traffic, which can quickly put a dent in even the best-laid plans. Since the Pacific Coast Highway is more or less the only way in and out of the city, daily rush hour snarls should be carefully scheduled around.

Photographs: top right and below by Silvia Mautner Photography; right ©iStockphoto.com/billyhoiler

Part of what makes Malibu such an ideal destination wedding spot is its easy proximity to so many other breathtaking areas—Santa Monica is perfect for a pre-wedding shopping spree with the girls or a rousing rehearsal dinner to help unite the new family. During the day in Malibu you can have your pick of water sports, such as enjoying one of America's top surfing spots and finding your balance on the waves. Those with balance of a different sort can join the parade of bicyclists and roller skaters who leisurely coast along the boardwalk, faces upturned to catch the sun. Some of the world's finest restaurants have recently opened their kitchens to the people of Malibu, and snagging a corner table next to a famous face makes for a meal your guests won't soon forget.

Photographs by Simone & Martin Photography, simonemartin.com

The mixture of Old Hollywood enchantment with a relaxed beach town vibe presents the perfect atmosphere for a wedding. Just as the early film stars were drawn to this magical place for its fascinating history and splendid natural beauty, today's couples can experience Malibu's enigmatic charms while feeling like the stars of their own show.

Photographs by Simone & Martin Photography, simonemartin.com

When it comes to venues...

I recommend touring Saddle Rock Ranch, which is part of Malibu Family Wines' estate and has a variety of different event-appropriate settings: a garden with the Santa Monica Mountains as the backdrop, a lakeside oak grove with great lawn, a stone château in the middle of the vineyards, and Camp Cabernet, which is a unique collection of chicly remodeled trailers ideal for luxurious lounging beside the grapevines. Rocky Oaks Estate is another breathtaking setting, comprising 37 acres of vineyards and citrus groves with a fabulous panoramic view of the ocean. If you're interested in a venue with a bit of French flavor, Church Estate Vineyards is absolutely exquisite; the château-style architecture and rolling landscape have a romantic ambience and storybook charm. Cull's Way is a 12-acre estate with three sides facing the water. It's the private residence of Dick Clark, so a personal referral is required to even tour the property, but if you're lucky enough to secure a date, guests will never forget the experience. Bel-Air Bay Club offers half a dozen distinct settings for events formal and casual alike; elegant rooms and vast expanses of lawn space accommodate groups from a couple dozen to more than a thousand.

Photographs courtesy of Church Estate Vineyards

Church Estate Vineyards
Enchanting. Idyllic. Timeless.

With its charming French château, majestic sycamore trees, rolling vineyards, and Monet-inspired gardens, Church Estate Vineyards bestows upon its visitors a wonderland of natural beauty and artistic nuances set atop the Malibu coastline. Offering exquisite outdoor entertaining throughout the year, Church Estate's 8.5 acres are a magical canvas on which to paint a picture of the perfect fairytale wedding.

Photographs: above and left by Starla Fortunato Photography; top left by Yvette Roman Photography

89

From the 300-year-old fountain that welcomes you upon arrival to the first-century stones from Cyprus that pave the 4,000-bottle wine cellar, authentic artifacts populate the grounds of Church Estate Vineyards. Entrepreneur and history aficionado Robert Church Haggstrom bought the property in 2003 and created a romantic enclave of Old World charm and of-the-moment sophistication. The estate's two-acre boutique vineyard of prized pinot noir and chardonnay grapes rolls along the hillside in bountiful rows colorfully framed by fragrant garden roses. Indoors, a true sojourn-in-Provence experience awaits, fostered by thoughtful details like the fine furnishings upholstered in toile and the charming French doors' antique Crémone hardware.

Photographs: below by Dahl Photography; right and bottom left by Starla Fortunato Photography; bottom right by Michael Segal Photography

Whether you yearn for an elegantly casual ceremony in the rustic boathouse accompanied by diving hummingbirds and gliding black and white swans or a formal reception in the magnificent, European-inspired château complete with a 15th-century French stone fireplace and 1911 Steinway grand piano, the vineyard can grant any wish.

Photographs: right by Michael Segal Photography; below by Miki and Sonja Photography; bottom right by Tauran Photography

When it comes to catering...

Wolfgang Puck Catering is a wonderful option if you're looking for a name that out-of-town guests will know and love; the celebrity caterer only serves the most exclusive regions in the country, and greater Malibu is all the better for it. Another caterer with a reputation as big as the flavors it creates is The Kitchen for Exploring Foods, a great choice for globally inspired cuisine. Most famous for its concept of lasagna cupcakes, Heirloom LA is led by a trio of self-proclaimed foodies who are always on the lookout for interesting ways to present their cuisine. Joan's on Third also has an amazing repertoire of crowd-pleasers, from appetizers like mini portobello mushroom quinoa cakes with curry sauce to desserts like marshmallow cloud cupcakes dipped in chocolate and an array of main courses and side dishes in between. Someone's in the Kitchen focuses on creative food that feeds the spirit and lingers in memory, which is exactly what wedding-goers look forward to.

Photographs: above courtesy of Wolfgang Puck Catering, by Cabriel Boone Photography; right courtesy of Joan's on Third

Joan's on Third
Bountiful. Family. Fresh.

Culinary enthusiast Joan McNamara has been building a flawless reputation and nourishing the appetites of Hollywood's celebrities and L.A.'s local food lovers since 1991, serving comfort food with a sophisticated twist. She perpetually seeks out exciting new ideas by traveling with her business partners, daughters Carol and Susie, and discovering regional specialties across the globe. They appreciate culinary fare of all sorts in a lifelong celebration of food, and sprinkle that passion into offerings such as prosciutto-wrapped halibut with fresh fig salsa or paper-thin grilled zucchini with citron goat cheese and fresh thyme. Along with her thriving marketplace and café, Joan has all her gourmet bases covered.

Photographs courtesy of Joan's on Third

Wolfgang Puck Catering
Seasonal. Innovative. Delicious.

On your big day you want guests to have an experience they'll never forget. Wolfgang Puck's signature catering services can accommodate any size, theme, or individual requirements—anywhere. Its award-winning chefs bring a superior level of creativity and flavor to the table. World-class cuisine and service are offered at one of the organization's landmark venues or a Malibu location that's special to you, even a romantic beachfront setting. Wolfgang's devotion to using only the freshest, highest-quality seasonal ingredients manifests on every plate. Wolfgang abides by his affirmation: "Heart and love inspire everything I do—these are the ingredients that make creating weddings our simplest pleasure." The team's commitment to personalized service and sustainable harvest will make you feel wonderful, inside and out.

Photographs: left by Cabriel Boone Photography; below and bottom left by Tracey Landworth Photography

When it comes to floral design...

Mark's Garden is a fine resource for star-quality floral creativity, best known for its work for awards shows, celebrity weddings, and television shows but equally popular among couples who simply have good taste. Amy Marella's studio The Hidden Garden is an excellent choice if you want a really personalized process that leads to fabulous floral designs; the owner describes her work by its essence, with categories like rich romance, sophisticated glamour, rustic elegance, and lush garden to name a few. I'm also quite fond of End Design, owned by Eden Rodriguez, known for its chic, edgy designs. Empty Vase offers an array of creative looks, whether working with mass quantities of a single type of flower or a variety of flowers in complementary color families. Likewise, Gilly Flowers & Events enjoys the task of being innovative within any genre of artistry, be it funky, sophisticated, traditional, or otherwise.

Photographs: above courtesy of Mark's Garden; top right courtesy of Empty Vase; right courtesy of The Hidden Garden, by John Solano Photography

Empty Vase
Brilliant. Stylish. Expertise.

The talented floral design and event production team at Empty Vase never seems to run out of imagination. Whether creating topiaries, elegantly potted vignettes, or floral arrangements bursting with vivid color, the studio's expert florists have an endless repertoire—it's no wonder their floral success has led them to full-scale event design. Empty Vase event coordinators are well-versed in creatively responding to even the most complex of design requests, which is one of the many reasons their work adorns high-profile weddings, celebrity parties, and other special events.

Photograph courtesy of Empty Vase

Instead of designing in advance, founder Saeed Babaeean and his team prefer to take their cues from the flowers as to how they should be arranged. The designers' backgrounds vary from fine art to fashion but all of the professionals find inspiration in an array of sources—store window fronts, newspaper articles, and everyday experiences. Insisting that emotions and visions are freely shared, they thrive on the challenge of designing anew each time, developing fabulous arrangements that precisely fit the event's tone, style, and theme.

Photographs courtesy of Empty Vase

Brides who long for petals with punch find their kindred spirits at gilly flowers & events, where the staff dreams up funky, romantic, and totally original creations that consistently satisfy every style and desire. From within the quaint shop emerge vibrant centerpieces, playful boutonnières, and storybook-perfect bouquets, all designed to elicit gasps of astonishment from the wedding party, the guests, and even random passers-by. Whether saturated, monochromatic rose balls or feathery, light-as-air floral confections, the flowers are always exactly, absolutely perfect.

Photographs by Laura Kleimhenz, Docuvitae

The Hidden Garden
Fresh. Vivid. Divine.

As stylish and creative as they are enthusiastic and personal, The Hidden Garden's designers know exactly how to fulfill a floral fantasy. Knowing when to scale back or heighten the drama is a delicate line the talented Hidden Garden team has been balancing masterfully for years. Whether it's a profusion of exotic blossoms or a clean arrangement of slender orchids, crafting floral décor that delights and surprises is the basis for their passion.

Photographs: right and below by John Solano Photography; bottom right by Joe Buissink

Mark's Garden
Renowned. Fabulous. Colorful.

Recreating a bride's fantasy of her wedding day is the goal of Mark Held each time he designs floral décor for the nuptial celebration. From the bridal bouquet to the ceremony and throughout the reception, his inspiringly artistic creations fulfill dreams to last a lifetime. Mark is consistently acclaimed for his trendsetting designs, unique floral selections, and innovative use of color.

Photographs: above by Yvette Roman Photography; top and bottom left by Richard David

When it comes to cakes and invitations…

Don't be shy about sampling or previewing dozens of options; it's one of the most enjoyable aspects of planning a wedding. For great taste and designs ranging from classic to outlandish, you'll definitely want to meet TV personality Duff Goldman, the mastermind behind Charm City Cakes, and his team of expert bakers and decorators. If you're into tradition, Hansen's Cakes boasts a legacy of delicious dessert recipes dating to 1520—yes, seven generations strong. While established more recently, Joanie & Leigh's Cake Divas is by no means short on recipes or inspiring concoctions; the flavors are fresh, and the presentation is exquisite. Fantasy Frostings lives up to its name with originals like the New Orleans spice cake, which is flavored with cinnamon, nutmeg, cloves, and a splash of brandy then filled with a soft cream mousse drizzled with caramel. For invitations, there's one company that I recommend above all the rest: Lehr & Black Invitationers. This stationer has absolutely revolutionized the art of invitations through beautiful workmanship and the use of fine papers, fabrics, and accent pieces.

Photographs: right courtesy of Mindy Weiss Party Consultants, by John Solano Photography; bottom right courtesy of Wolfgang Puck Catering, by Gabriel Boone Photography; right, below, bottom right courtesy of Church Estate Vineyards

When it comes to preserving memories...

There is no shortage of talent, so I think the most important thing is to choose professionals whose personalities put you at ease. Regardless of setting or subject, a sexy timelessness pervades all of Simone & Martin Photography's portraiture, ensuring that everyone looks their absolute best. Elizabeth Messina is known for her romantic approach to the art form and travels pretty extensively to shoot destination weddings throughout Southern California and internationally. I'm also a fan of Yitzhak Dalal, whose cinematic style and background in fashion form a winning combination for naturally giving brides and grooms the glamorous look of celebrities. Jay Lawrence Goldman is passionate about weddings but also does quite a bit of commercial work, giving him a particularly broad perspective and toolbox of techniques. In the way of videography, Vidicam Productions is an excellent resource for creating heirloom quality films that can take on a variety of aesthetics—from Old Hollywood to contemporary chic—all captured in high definition, of course.

Photographs: above left and left by Jay Lawrence Goldman Photography; above right by Elizabeth Messina Photography

Elizabeth Messina Photography
Lovely. Grace. Intuition.

Elizabeth Messina is an artist and happily married mother of three. With endorsements from Brooke Shields, Tori Spelling, and Kate Walsh, she has certainly attracted a discriminating clientele. Capturing the nuances of love and affection is her way of bringing a little more beauty and sweetness into the world. When Elizabeth is not photographing other people's love stories, she is tending to her own in the sun-kissed setting of Southern California.

Photographs by Elizabeth Messina Photography

Elizabeth's innate sense of style and graceful demeanor are reflected in her photographs as well as in her book *The Luminous Portrait*, which eloquently reveals the secrets to her creative approach. She is enamored with travel and photographs weddings from coast to coast and throughout the Caribbean and Europe. Wherever she goes, Elizabeth will undoubtedly be loading film in her camera and capturing joy, laughter, and the beauty of life.

Photographs by Elizabeth Messina Photography

Jay Lawrence Goldman Photography
Treasure. Emotion. Bright.

Having photographed countless weddings and made guest appearances on "America's Next Top Model," Jay Goldman is a well-known expert on art and style. You can tell how passionate he is by the way he describes the process of capturing the magical moment when a woman goes from fiancée to bride—nothing matches the glow she has about her. He truly sees the world in a way that others can only understand through his photographs, and that perspective and artistry are what make each collection of wedding images entirely unique and special.

Photographs by Jay Lawrence Goldman Photography

Duke's Malibu
Picturesque. Inviting. Memorable.

Known as much for his charm and integrity as for his prowess in the water, Duke Paoa Kahanamoku embodied the true meaning of "aloha." Besides winning numerous Olympic swimming medals and catapulting the sport of surfing to new heights, this Waikiki beach boy managed to always remain gracious and grounded, even when Hollywood came calling. His friendly spirit is embodied at Duke's Malibu, one of five beachside restaurants in California and Hawaii dedicated to honoring Hawaii's most famous citizen.

Photographs: right and below courtesy of Duke's Malibu; bottom right by Bella Pictures

The gorgeous, sweeping views of the Pacific provide the perfect atmosphere for old friends and new family to mix, be it during the wedding reception, rehearsal dinner, day-after brunch, or even the ceremony itself. The Moana Room offers a private oasis from the main restaurant, complete with its own entrance and bridal suite. Two walls of floor-to-ceiling windows showcasing the crashing waves just outside, along with a deck overlooking the sand, make this a one-of-a-kind setting. Here you can create a casual celebration or transform the room into an elegant affair limited only by your imagination.

Photographs by Josh Derek

Duke's menus feature an extensive selection of customizable plated, buffet, or family-style options, including a variety of fresh, sustainable seafood and premium steaks. When you desire to treat guests to an oceanfront experience, Duke's Malibu provides the ideal spot for friendly, memorable gatherings.

Photographs courtesy of Duke's Malibu

Resource One Inc.
Fabric. Personality. Statement.

Imagine luxury linens, decorative décor, and crystal-clear ghost chairs all available at one wonderful location. Roberta Karsch's amazing team at Resource One Inc. are enthusiastic wedding specialists, providing full design services to hotels, floral designers, and wedding planners. Most of all, they love to work closely with each bride to assist in creating a beautiful environment for her very special event. From a Malibu beachfront wedding in the sand to an A-list dinner in an exquisite private home, Resource One Inc. is the premier name for luxury linens. Have the perfect napkin, charger, tablecloth, and chair treatment delivered to your venue for the picture-perfect wedding celebration.

Photographs: above by Barber Photography; left by Duke Photography

Orange County
by Jeannie Savage, Details Details

Southern California's Orange County has a claim to fame. With the ever-growing popularity of television shows and movies filmed in OC presenting its aura of affluence and relaxed American lifestyle, the region has grown more celebrated than ever, drawing tourists from all over the United States and the world. It's home to legendary oceanfront communities and their world-renowned resorts, top-rated beaches, and historic attractions like Mission San Juan Capistrano with its gently tolling bells. No wonder Orange County has become a destination wedding paradise. I love it with all my heart!

One thing that is most alluring to visitors of Orange County is its envied Mediterranean climate, making it a perfect year-round setting for destination weddings and outdoor celebrations. From sunset ceremonies overlooking the Pacific to glamorous receptions in luxurious landmark hotels, Orange County offers its residents and fortunate tourists awe-inspiring natural beauty and sophistication all at once.

Photographs by Hoffmann Photographer

It's simply smart to host your wedding in Orange County, with access to high-end retail shopping, award-winning restaurants, and charming cafes. There's Corona Del Mar, Laguna Beach, Newport Beach, Huntington Beach, and the South Coast Plaza shopping mecca. You can explore 24 miles of beautiful beaches for surfing, strolling, and scuba diving. At Fashion Island, the Balboa Peninsula, and downtown Laguna Beach, luxury stores and boutiques abound along with casual and fine dining to suit every taste. Orange County also offers museums and the performing arts are world-class. Bringing the wedding party, family, and friends to OC can only mean one thing: fun for everyone!

Photographs: right by John & Joseph Photography; below by Ira Lippke Studios; bottom right by Sarah K. Chen

People can be entertained according to their interests. Beyond the world-famous theme parks such as Disneyland, there are numerous attractions—Disney California Adventure, Fun Zone at Balboa Peninsula, and Discovery Science Center among others—for the entire family to enjoy on an extended vacation after the wedding. For those who love the sea, Dana Point offers fishing boat trips and whale-watching excursions, and Laguna Beach boasts surfing lessons. Pampering the wedding party is an Orange County specialty, with hotel spas and spa cuisine to delight the ladies, while a round of ocean-view championship golf for the guys makes for a great bonding experience.

Getting here is easy for wedding guests. John Wayne Airport serves all of Orange County from its convenient location adjacent to Newport Beach and Irvine. It's not congested like LAX, making transportation for out-of-towners smooth as silk. Besides, who wants the added stress of Los Angeles freeways when you're trying to make it to the church on time?

Photographs: above left by Robert Evans; above right by Joe Latter Photographer; right by Samuel Lippke Studios

We love doing highly personalized celebrations. One East Coast bride was an accomplished synchronized swimmer, so we hosted her wedding event at a private estate replete with sparkling swimming pool. During the cocktail hour, a performance of synchronized swimmers wowed guests and made the whole event all about the bride. A Las Vegas couple wanted to escape the summer's scorching desert heat, so we designed their beachfront wedding at Montage Laguna Beach with billowing canopies for the lawn ceremony, then dinner and dancing under the stars.

The diverse mix of cultures in Orange County offers a vast array of ethnic restaurants and dining choices from Italian to Chinese and everything in between, like classic steakhouses and fresh seafood places. Rehearsal dinners are often themed to match the restaurant; we designed one such dinner as a relaxed and joyful celebration with authentic Mexican fare and traditional costumed mariachis!

Photographs: above by Ira Lippke Studios; right by Braedon Photography; facing page by Barber Photography

We specialize in helping brides who live out of state or in foreign countries, designing multiple-day events and offering full-service coordination from beginning to end. One bride from Japan had us handle all the details and design the entire affair, so she could simply step into her magical wedding!

We have an insider's approach to organizing and managing the nuptial ceremony and full reception, plus pre- and post- festivities like rehearsal dinners, excursions, brunches, and late-night afterparties. Orange County is the ideal spot to produce elegant and unforgettable wedding events. With meticulous planning and a passion for perfection, your big day will be full of color, texture, and imagination.

Photographs: top left by John & Joseph Photography; top right by Jessica Claire; left by Samuel Lippke Studios; facing page by Victor Sizemore

When it comes to hotels...

Finding a luxurious landmark in Pacific Coast paradise is a breeze. If you want to experience oceanfront rooms with spectacular cliffside views and Spanish Colonial interiors, Montage Laguna Beach is the place to enjoy classic California ambience. The awe-inspiring St. Regis Monarch Beach on beautiful Dana Point offers signature style with a gracious staff and world-class amenities to fulfill every need. The Ritz-Carlton, Laguna Niguel is serene and sophisticated and known for a legacy of extraordinary service as well as a dedication to conserving its natural surroundings. The Resort at Pelican Hill is perched on 504 acres overlooking crashing waves in sunny Newport Beach, a dramatic setting that will captivate you and your wedding party.

Photographs courtesy of Montage Laguna Beach

Montage Laguna Beach
Seaside. Artful. Pleasures.

Californians agree. Montage Laguna Beach has a character and elegance all its own. The storied oceanfront destination surrounded by a renowned artistic community has beckoned millions of travelers and locals to its timeless Craftsman-style architecture perched high on a cliff—a picturesque estate to call home for an extended stay, restorative vacation, special event, or pampering weekend getaway.

Photographs courtesy of Montage Laguna Beach

Destination weddings take on new meaning at Montage Laguna Beach. Beyond luxury accommodations, the resort offers amenities and a dedicated service staff so you can rest assured that every detail will be attended to for a perfect visit. Guestrooms offer sophisticated turn-of-the-century décor and subtle color schemes that backdrop early California artwork. Your private ocean-view balcony or patio brings the beauty of the outdoors in, while 100-percent Egyptian cotton towels and plush robes wrap you in comfort each time you step out of the well-appointed marble bathroom. Spa Montage is at your service for soothing massages and treatments to de-stress and beautify before wedding festivities, and resort activities abound for fitness as well as relaxation. Enjoy a full-circuit workout, a swim in the pool, or a revitalizing beachfront yoga class with breathtaking views stretching from every vantage point. Being in the idyllic Laguna Beach location invites you to go gallery hopping, surfing, or simply bask in ideal sunny weather—the choice is yours. Just imagine the photo opportunities!

Photographs courtesy of Montage Laguna Beach

Food for the soul is a promise. Acclaimed chefs Craig Strong, Rob Wilson, and Casey Overton form the award-winning Montage culinary team, ready to prepare modern French and American cuisine or design personalized menus for seated dinners, cocktail parties, and brunches. Highlighting delicious artisanal ingredients and alluring boutique wines, chefs can create a mouthwatering wedding feast with a mélange of flavors that tastes as wonderful as it looks. Overlooking the blue Pacific, Studio at Montage consistently presents a delectable dining experience in a comfortably elegant atmosphere, while The Loft serves breakfast, lunch, and dinner in a fresh, decidedly California style with stunning ocean views that go on forever. Capturing your senses and making your dreams come true is the art of Montage Laguna Beach—a blissful place that inspires once-in-a-lifetime romantic memories.

Photographs courtesy of Montage Laguna Beach

When it comes to venues...

Hosting your ceremony and reception in unexpected places is the latest trend, and Orange County has some of the finest spaces with creative possibilities for the ultimate destination experience. "Unlimited" is the best word to describe the original Seven-Degrees venue, a blank canvas that allows your ceremony and reception to exhibit an artistic edge entirely customized to your liking. Impressive and refined, The Richard Nixon Presidential Library offers unmatched splendor for elegant parties, especially when held in the formal ballroom. If you dream of a rustic and elegant affair on a private estate under centuries-old oaks, Rancho Las Lomas provides an intimate, picturesque atmosphere on its lovingly restored property amid botanical and zoological gardens.

Photographs courtesy of Seven-Degrees, by Nicole Caldwell

[Seven-Degrees]
Innovative. Limitless. Stunning.

The number "7" conjures up many associations: seven days of the week, the Seven Wonders of the World, lucky number seven. For art and event venue [seven-degrees], the number refers mainly to the architectural angles found throughout the building's design. Nestled in the downtown Laguna Beach arts district, the two-building, 25,000-square-foot space houses not only indoor and outdoor locations specifically built for entertaining, but also an art gallery and artists' work-live studios.

DeeDee Anderson and Mark Orgill, co-founders of [seven-degrees], bought the property, designed the space, and spent over three years building it. The outcome is a fresh and entirely original approach to art and celebrations—it's like a big sculpture that's constantly changing. Your wedding will be as unique as you are in such an inspiring space, from edgy to elegant; the creative choices are all yours.

Photographs by Nicole Caldwell

The in-house team of event and wedding experts at [seven-degrees] can deftly design, plan, and produce, as well as provide catering, florals, and décor. The 4,500-square-foot Media Lounge, with its rotating art exhibits, is extremely versatile. A fully integrated LED lighting system, zoned sound system, mounted flat panel video displays, retractable large screen video projection systems, and live feed video cameras give you a wide array of technological toys to play with. And special outdoor areas offer unexpected romantic vignettes and photo opportunities—the hillside terrace and en plein air balcony are one-of-a-kind.

Led by executive director Dora Wexell, the team employs a collaborative approach with wedding hosts, involving the bride and groom in the whole process while coaxing out their inner artistes. Sometimes resident artists also give input, bringing their ideas and daring perspective to the table. Teamwork is only one of the venue's set of creative elements, which also includes emphasis on design, technology, and connection.

Photographs by Nicole Caldwell

Like an artist's broad stroke concept, your [seven-degrees] wedding is filled with limitless potential and a spectrum of possibilities. The Wedding Curation Team will involve you in the creative process from day one, listening to your vision and guiding you in designing a ceremony and reception to fit your personal aesthetic. The result is a wedding that celebrates the joy of the day, feels thematically consistent, and looks truly stunning. Whether avant-garde, traditional, contemporary, or a combination thereof, each wedding is a bespoke work of art.

The seven elements of the [seven-degrees] wedding present a colorful palette for exploration. There are endless ways in which you can customize your wedding experience. And like the artist at her easel, creativity is boundless, fueled by your own vivid imagination with our painter's box of expertise at hand.

Photographs by Nicole Caldwell

When it comes to catering...

In Orange County, award-winning culinary pros abound to satisfy the most discerning palates. An Catering takes a family tradition of creating tasty food to a whole new level. The chefs at Good Gracious put fun and love into their menu planning and create savory dishes using natural slow cooking and green-minded methods. Perfectionism and a passion for excellence is what 24 Carrots brings to the table, offering flawless cuisine and full-service event production. Jay's Catering promises a delicious mix of tradition and innovation with spectacular food, dazzling presentations, and creative themes. Crème de la Crème Gourmet Foods & Catering is known for mouthwatering menus including passed hors d'oeuvres such as phyllo purses filled with smoked salmon and leeks and entrée creations like sirloin of lamb with thyme-scented jus and ratatouille.

Photographs: right courtesy of An Catering, by Eric Raptosh; below courtesy of Crème de la Crème, byTony Sanders; bottom right courtesy of Good Gracious, by Marianne Lozano Photography

An Catering
Simple. Natural. Refined.

Mouthwatering taste and minimalist presentation are what you can expect from An Catering: gourmet food that appeals to all of the senses. With executive chef Helene An at the helm and spearheaded by her daughter Catherine, An Catering finds an artful balance of taste and creativity that will leave your guests craving more. The An family is known throughout Orange County by way of their gourmet noodle bar, AnQi Bistro, where you can dine on a fashion catwalk designed by House of An's chief executive officer Elizabeth An. AnQi serves as a satellite kitchen for An Catering, where the family's passion for style and meticulously prepared food makes it a standout.

Photographs: left by Mario Sanchez; below by Alex Vasilescu

When it comes to floral design...

Your celebration deserves fantastic blossoms from all over the globe. Orange County offers top picks for creative floral designs, from hand-tied bouquets to lavish centerpieces that enhance the nuptial ceremony and add fragrant beauty to your reception. Christopher Aldama of Fiori Fresco Special Events will "paint" your vision by producing one-of-a-kind weddings, whether themed or custom-built, and Sunny Ravanbach's White Lilac premier studio will ensure that your total environment surpasses expectations, designed to your color scheme and inspired by your imagination and style. Nisie's Enchanted Florist designs truly unique and breathtaking arrangements, all in good taste. And Bloom Box creates lush and stylized displays for an exclusive and glamorous floral look that reflects you perfectly.

Photographs: above courtesy of White Lilac, by Devin Pense; top left courtesy of Bloom Box, by Global Photography; left courtesy of Christopher Aldama, Fiori Fresco Special Events

Bloom Box
Environments. Nirvana. Glamour.

Creating floral environments—this is the specialty of Bloom Box, one of Orange County's best kept secrets. Fayaz Chamadia's boutique studio designs and produces a multitude of glamorous and stylized events, with über chic weddings highlighting its vast portfolio of artistic custom work. Imagine having your dream wedding alive with vivid color, sensual fragrance, and an exclusive lush display that is personalized to your particular taste.

Photographs: top by Samuel Lippke Studios; above by Hoffman Photographer; left by Barber Photography

Your floral environment, most importantly, should define the mood and express your true persona, while transporting guests to a magical place filled with a sense of intimacy. Beyond table arrangements, nuptial adornments, and bridal bouquets setting the scene, Bloom Box also provides unique rentals, eclectic décor, and bespoke prop fabrication to complete a tailored look. Fayaz and his talented team style your wedding for an unparalleled ambience, from the ceremony to the reception and throughout pre- and post-wedding festivities.

Photographs: below and bottom by Andrena Photography; right by Lin and Jirsa Photography

Christopher Aldama, Fiori Fresco Special Events
Exceptional. Personal. Comprehensive.

Your Southern California wedding is bound to be exceptional when Christopher Aldama of Fiori Fresco Special Events is your co-host. From theming and planning to décor, catering, photographers, floral, entertainment, and every last detail, Fiori Fresco works to create a personalized vision that reflects your taste and style. Whether your dream wedding is an intimate gathering of close family and friends, a destination event in an exotic port of call, or a lavish spread for 1,000 guests, it will be a celebration that fully expresses you.

Photographs: above by Withers Wanberg; top left by Ira Lippke Studios; left by Victor Sizemore

Fiori Fresco calls upon the best in the business and knows the coveted venues and wedding professionals to help make your rehearsal dinner, ceremony, reception, and after-party, once-in-a-lifetime experiences. Christopher Aldama draws upon creative talents, award-winning reputation, culinary arts and business degrees, and vast experience to assemble an attentive team that handles it all so you can relax and be stress-free. You simply provide the inspiration and your story, while the Fiori Fresco crew manifests a celebration that is truly impressive and a reflection of you and the things you care about. The talented design and production team have access to top resources with proven experience to create anything your heart desires on an intimate or grand scale.

Photographs: right by Ira Lippke Studios; below by Withers Wanberg; bottom right by John & Joseph Photography

Walking hand in hand with each couple, the Fiori Fresco staff leads you through making the right choices so you get what means the most to you, your family, and guests on your wedding day. They understand how special this milestone is, and how important it is for this day to be very personal—an unexpected gift for you and yours to enjoy!

Photographs: right by Withers Wanberg; below by Joe Photo; bottom right by Ira Lippke Studios

White Lilac
Original. Inspired. Admired.

White Lilac's director of design Sunny Ravanbach is a creative fountain of ideas. She has an innate talent for designing some of Southern California's most talked about galas, weddings, and soirées. From the very first meeting with this talented entrepreneur, you'll discover her passion for turning the simplest inspiration, perhaps your favorite color, into a personalized venue theme: your wedding dream come true. From tabletop décor to linens and draping to florals and lighting, Sunny loves to walk with you through the decision-making process. Your wedding celebration will be impeccable and beautiful, but most of all, original.

Photographs by Devin Pense

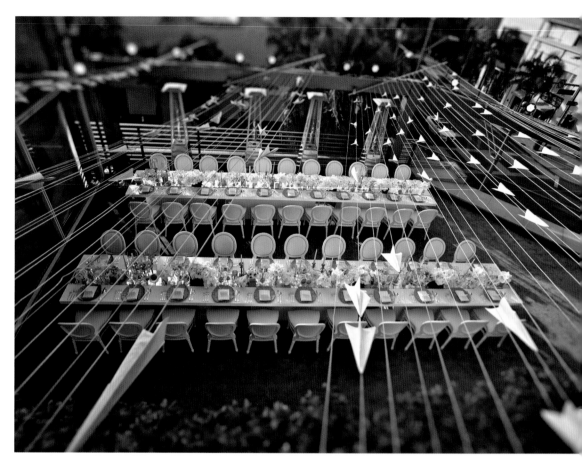

When it comes to cakes and invitations…

Orange County has a bevy of talented bakers who can create delicious tiers and stationers who can develop luxury announcements. Filigree Cakes personalizes cakes that express your taste in couture style, while Heslington Cakes creates tiers a French chef would envy with flawless fondant and sugar art techniques. Let Them Eat Cake whips up confections from scratch using organic ingredients for 100-percent edible, towering creations. Details À La Carte experts are your go-to invitation gurus with fine papers and distinctive inks that announce festivities with classic grace, a lighthearted touch, or a modern vibe. Want something different? Rock Paper Scissors designs gorgeous three-dimensional "gift box" invitations and clever announcements like specially printed wine bottle corks as save-the-dates.

Photographs: above courtesy of Details À La Carte, by Jessica Claire; left courtesy of Heslington Cakes, LLC, by Sara Heslington

Details À La Carte
Refined. Tactile. Individual.

First impressions are everything. At Details À La Carte, Nichelle Luc has mastered the art of the invitation, the romantic prelude to the celebration and wedding festivities to come. She uses fine papers and distinctive ink processes, as well as materials such as wood, fabric, and acrylic, to create custom announcements, save-the-dates, invitations, programs, placecards, table numbers, menus, and thank-you notes that personalize your wedding from start to finish. Nichelle's penchant for beautiful papers and font styles is apparent in every carefully crafted design made to echo the color scheme or theme—whether clean and modern, fun and stylish, or classic and elegant—assuring that the visual impact of each piece expresses your uniqueness.

Photographs: left by Jasmine Star Photography; below by Jessica Claire; bottom left by Samuel Lippke Studios

Filigree Cakes
Specialty. Baked. Lovely.

In 2001, Sunny Lee switched her career from flight attendant to cake decorating expert. She discovered her innate creative talent studying at the Culinary Academy in San Francisco, graduating at the top of the class, and then honed her technique working in pastry kitchens at The Ritz-Carlton in Laguna Niguel and the Bellagio in Las Vegas, founding Filigree Cakes in Orange County seven years later.

Brides-to-be know Sunny by name and flock to her cake design shop, ordering specialty confections in flavors and styles personalized to the chosen theme or color scheme. Elegant, extravagant, and everything in-between, Filigree Cakes is synonymous with handcrafted artistry and grace. Sunny's tiered cake designs tower and impress. Baked from scratch, each creation is a vision of scrumptiousness covered in fondant and decorated with sugar art and gum paste flowers. Lovely to behold and delicious to taste, Filigree Cakes' creations promise a sweet grand finale to your wedding feast.

Photographs: top left by Ira Lippke Studios; left and below by SimplyTwo Photography

Heslington Cakes, LLC
Sublime. Detailed. Floral.

Sara Heslington creates expressive cakes worthy of a regal wedding. Her artistry was honed at New York's French Culinary Institute's pastry chef program. Teaming with renowned NYC cake designer Ron Ben-Israel and working as an assistant pastry chef at boutique hotels catapulted this stylist into opening her own cake design gallery in 2010. Tiered cakes covered in flawless rolled fondant and decorated with handcrafted sugar flowers are Sara's specialty. Her gum paste florals are so amazing you'd think they are real blooms. Even finishing touches of royal icing lace, lattice, and scrollwork exude elegance, gracing luscious fresh-baked layers in flavors ready to please the most sophisticated palate.

Photographs by Sara Heslington

When it comes to preserving memories...

John & Joseph Photography takes a photojournalistic approach, capturing those special romantic moments filled with emotional nuances. Samuel Lippke shoots images exhibiting artistic flair, fashion attitude, and a certain edge with his documentary storytelling style. I'm fond of Jessica Claire's work because it is always fresh, real, beautiful, and as she says, "just like reality... with a punch!" Victor Sizemore gives new meaning to feelings of love in his happy engagement and wedding portraits that exude each couple's marriage of personalities. International photographer Jasmine Star makes you the celebrity of the day, working to discover your uniqueness in every posed or candid shot.

Photographs: above by John Hong and Joseph Hong; left by Samuel Lippke Studios

John & Joseph
Journalistic. Memorable. Art.

Want your wedding story told creatively with a decidedly new perspective? There are two names you need to remember: John and Joseph. If ever Oscar Wilde's quote of "life imitates art more than art imitates life" applied, it is through the engaging images captured by brothers John and Joseph Hong, Southern California's acclaimed photojournalistic team. Refreshingly unconventional yet timeless, their artistic approach is all about preserving special moments, from shared emotions to a private glance, your glowing beauty to natural scenery—all of the nuances and details surrounding you and the people you love.

Photographs by John Hong and Joseph Hong

Samuel Lippke Studios
Creative. Fashion. Story.

Through his unique lens, Samuel Lippke loves to tell a story. Imagine your wedding story told through creative images shot in a photojournalistic style with a dash of fashion attitude. A Washington state native, Samuel studied photography and worked alongside his photographer brother before stepping into his namesake Samuel Lippke Studios. Today he shoots for high-profile clientele in Southern California and throughout the U.S. as one of the highly respected talents in the business.

Photographs by Samuel Lippke Studios

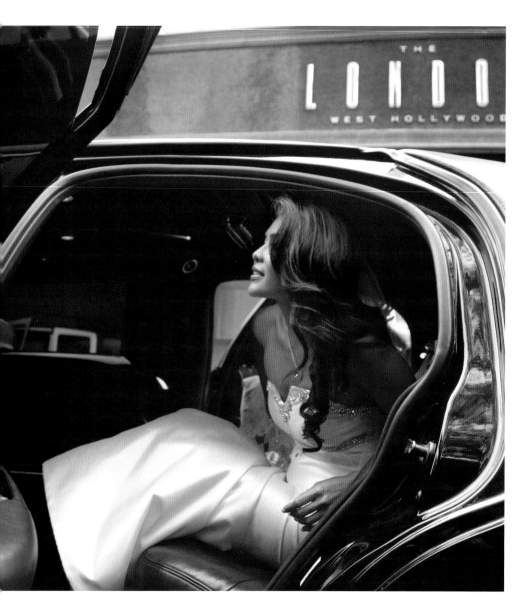

Meeting Samuel Lippke in person or perusing his uncut blog gives you a feel for the man who makes brides and grooms the focus of attention. Whether color or black and white, each image has a fine art quality destined to become a family heirloom. Edgy, emotional, fashion-forward, architectural, natural, mood-enhancing; these are a few of the words that describe Samuel's amazing documentary storytelling style. Through his expert eye for capturing candid shots and arranging proper poses, your most romantic memories will be etched forever.

Photographs by Samuel Lippke Studios

Beauty by Berit
Radiant. Flawless. Stunning.

Blushing brides know her by name: Berit. She's the dedicated pro who promises wedding day radiance that turns heads. Berit's flawless bridal makeup techniques include airbrush application that lasts through a demanding day. Her experience of beautifying a hundred brides each year since 2006 makes Berit the go-to artist throughout Southern California. Traveling from her Laguna Beach studio, Berit is with you all day from dressing room to reception, for makeup touchups and a day-to-evening transformation. Romantic, retro, sunkissed, or glam—it's entirely your choice. She also offers elegant hairstyles to complete the portrait-perfect look. Berit is the bridal party's best friend, also enhancing mothers, attendants, and flower girl faces so they stay photo-ready through tears of joy, smiles, hugs, and kisses!

Photographs: above by Aaron Delesie; top left by Digs Studio; left by Lane Dittoe; all hair design by Tiffany Monday

Lighten Up
Powerful. Technical. Ambience.

Lighting makes any event magical and memorable. And getting married is one of the most exciting times of your life so your wedding celebration should rise to the occasion. From ceremony to cocktail hour and throughout the reception, Lighten Up designs the party atmosphere in harmony with your overall vision. Both intimate gatherings and large-scale affairs can be enhanced with creative pin spots, glowing lanterns, gobo designs, dance floor and stage lighting, architectural and landscape highlights—whatever is needed to set the mood.

Photographs courtesy of Lighten Up, Inc.

Sunset Cove Villas
Luxury. Oceanfront. Vacation.

Imagine being in friendly Laguna Beach, known for its artist colony heritage, film star legends, and rugged ocean coastline, experiencing an exotic island atmosphere in one of eight distinctively styled villas: Majorca, Laguna, Antigua, Martinique, Seychelles, Calypso, Djakarta, or Lanai. Available for an extended stay or weekend getaways, Sunset Cove Villas accommodations are located in the heart of Laguna Beach and offer awe-inspiring Pacific views, luxurious amenities, and privacy. Of course, there's also private access to Sleepy Hollow Beach and pristine sundecks, where basking in the sun and watching the crashing waves will be the only things on your agenda. Should you choose to venture out, you will find fine dining, shopping, and galleries just outside your villa.

Photographs: right and bottom right by Chet Frohlich; below by Mark Orgill

Palm Springs

by Kristin Banta, Kristin Banta Events

Frank Sinatra, Marilyn Monroe, and Bob Hope all knew: Palm Springs is a special place. Said to be "sprinkled with stardust" because of the waves of celebrities that have made the city their winter playground, it has long been an enclave for those seeking natural glamour to go along with their rest and relaxation. Located a mere two-hour drive from Hollywood, the ease of getting to and enjoying Palm Springs is only one of its many fantastic features.

For me, this has always been the perfect getaway spot. It has the feel of a full destination experience without the logistical madness that comes with international travel. Perhaps that's why Elvis and Priscilla Presley honeymooned here, or why President Eisenhower and his Mamie leased a house to escape to in the winter. Either way, the mountain ranges, stunning desert landscapes, and nearly perfect weather make reveling in your surroundings easy, whether your plans include a round of golf or nothing more taxing than a few days spent lounging by the pool. And I can hardly imagine a more beautiful setting for a wedding.

Photographs: above ©iStockphoto.com/LPETTET; facing page ©iStockphoto.com/2HotBrazil

and many homes and buildings constructed in that style still exist. Plenty of hotels and resorts pick up on this vibe, but each manages to remain wonderfully distinctive in its overall atmosphere. The sheer number of venues available in this resort town means that you can always find exactly the one to suit your personality. Each location strives to create

Even though it was established centuries ago by the Agua Caliente Cahuilla Indians and officially incorporated in 1938, Palm Springs maintains the mod, mid-century atmosphere it first became famous for—clean lines, striking architecture, and a sense of simple elegance throughout. The design aesthetic known as Desert Modernism originated here,

Photographs: above by Llanes Weddings; right by Memories by Michael

a comprehensive experience, helping you to forget about schedules and focus instead on the people who have gathered together for your wedding. The idea is to nestle in, shut out all the distractions from everyday life, and live your fairytale.

Photographs: top and right by Llanes Weddings; above by Memories by Michael

This ease of planning extends to your vendors as well. Since Palm Springs is so near to Los Angeles, you can still engage all your favorite vendors to create the customized experience you had imagined, or if it's more of a simplified day you are planning, you can always utilize the willing staff at your venue. Since I love to vacation here myself, I've developed close relationships over the years with the experts at several venues, both on a personal and professional level. The pride that everyone holds for the area is evident in the abundant recommendations for tours, restaurants, and other recreational activities. Whether you want to follow

Photographs: left by Alex Abercrombie Photographer; below © YourWeddingDay/Alyssa Nicol Photography; bottom left by Yvette Roman Photography; facing page by Kerry Corcoran, David Michael Photography

the Walk of Stars downtown, take in the spectacular desert views from the world's largest cable cars on the Palm Springs Aerial Tramway, or simply stick close to your resort, everyone wants to make sure you fully enjoy your time here. The breezy attitude is contagious, too—and that's something that every couple can appreciate. One celebrity wedding I designed here had the feel of a gypsy tent village, with flowing Moroccan fabrics and eclectic nautical treasures scattered about to help set the romantic, bohemian scene. Not only was the effect lush and exotic, but there was a tempered level of glitz that relaxed what, for most, can sometimes teeter on the brink of an overly formal occasion. Instead, the wedding was a serene, sexy event that perfectly reflected its surroundings.

Photographs by Miki & Sonja Photography

Palm Springs may have first gained notoriety thanks to Hollywood's "two-hour rule"—that all actors must remain within a two-hour drive of the studios in case of re-shoots—but today that short distance disguises its most alluring facet: that even though you haven't traveled far, you can still feel like you're a million miles away.

Photographs: right by Niki Delacueva; below by Llanes Weddings; bottom right by Laura Kleinhenz, Docuvitae

When it comes to hotels...

Korakia Pension has a really wonderful Mediterranean ambience in the rooms and throughout all of the indoor-outdoor common spaces; it even offers an authentic Moroccan tea service each afternoon. I also like Parker Palm Springs' beautifully appointed accommodations and the hotel's way of encouraging guests to enjoy the outdoors through a casual game of croquet, tennis, or pétanque. Known for its modern take on the alluring Hollywood Regency style, Viceroy Palm Springs Resort and Spa has three shimmering pools, just part of its claim to fame. If you're looking for a more laid-back setting, The Ace Hotel is eco-minded, dog-friendly, and bursting with fun activities for all ages.

Photographs: left courtesy of Viceroy Palm Springs; bottom left courtesy of Parker Palm Springs, by Nikolas Koenig; below courtesy of Parker Palm Springs

Parker Palm Springs
Fun. Beauty. Diverse.

Just as its sister property Le Parker Méridien New York echoes the qualities of its chic city locale, The Parker Palm Springs exudes the elegance and glamour of star-studded Southern California. From the historic Gene Autry residence or one of the luxury suites to a patio room that entices you to stay outdoors or a more basic estate room—entirely elegant, yet smaller and more suitable for those who will spend most of their time away from the hotel—options absolutely abound. Don't let the fabulous Jonathan Adler décor deceive you. While this is indeed a place for opulent relaxation, it's really a destination for every occasion: a leisurely weekend of croquet and pétanque, a dream wedding, or anything in between.

Photographs courtesy of Parker Palm Springs

Viceroy Palm Springs
Dramatic. Inspiring. Gracious.

Called "sleekly sexy" by *The New York Times*, dubbed "desert fabulousness" by *Bon Appetit*, and voted one of the top 50 hotel spas by *Condé Nast Traveler*, Viceroy Palm Springs Resort and Spa recaptures a Hollywood Regency style that provides a glamorous setting along with inspired accommodations and acclaimed service. Three courtyards with pools and lush gardens create a stunning backdrop for walking arm-in-arm with that special someone, lounging after a dip in the water, or relaxing after a gourmet dinner at Citron. The full-service Estrella Spa offers revitalizing and relaxing treatments, as well as personalized programs in a serene indoor-outdoor setting. But other activities, from golf to shopping, beckon visitors as well. Whether staying in a deluxe room, suite, or private villa, Viceroy Palm Springs is the ultimate escape.

Photographs by Grey Crawford

When it comes to catering...

You can't go wrong with Savore Cuisine & Events, known for its deep-rooted philosophy of continual reinvention, renewal, and rethinking in order to stay fabulous and on the cutting edge of the culinary scene. I also really like Jackson Somerset, which is celebrated for menu items that are as beautiful as they are tasty. If you want to introduce your guests to a Southern California institution, consider going with An Catering, a family-owned enterprise that has maintained a personal touch despite its rapid expansion.

Photographs courtesy of Savore Cuisine & Events, by Erez Levy

An Catering
Scrumptious. Exotic. Legacy.

With a solid reputation for its restaurants Crustacean, AnQi, and Tiato, An Catering brings style and gastronomical experience to every event. Helene An, matriarch and executive chef, spent much of her free time as a child in the kitchen with her family's Chinese, French, and Vietnamese chefs, absorbing their cultural differences and culinary techniques. Through her own global travels, daughter Catherine keeps An Catering innovative, fresh, and full of diverse flavors. Additionally, Catherine insists on only using the freshest, seasonally appropriate ingredients while striving to use the greenest alternatives possible. An Catering's crew of visual stylists and designers promise an impeccable presentation.

Photographs by Alex Vasilescu

Savore Cuisine & Events
Flavor. Artistry. Chic.

To Erez Levy and Richard Lauter, chef-owners of Savore Cuisine & Events, Palm Springs and its environs are a mere extension of the desert that is Los Angeles. Their gastronomic delights and event designs have starred in the most desirable and exclusive venues, such as Korakia Pension, The O'Donnell House, The Sinatra House, Big Horn, The Hideaway, Tamarisk, The Tradition, and The Madison, just to name a few. With a passion for cutting-edge culinary theory, Savore creates menus that are artful, seasonal, and stylish, but always focused on flavor. Wedding catering is elevated to new heights of personalization—a comprehensive process that includes methodical menu and service planning, bride and groom interviews, and menu tastings that feel more like sophisticated dinner parties.

Photographs by Erez Levy, Savore Cuisine & Events

When it comes to floral design...

The R. Jack Balthazar creative team takes events to new heights with their approach of using florals and other inspired decor to tell a story. Mille Fiori Floral Design knows how to spice up any occasion, whether a single arrangement for a loved one or a room bursting with floral designs to immediately establish an appropriately opulent ambience. I also recommend looking into Krista Jon's designs, which are sculptural, unique, and charming.

Photographs: right courtesy of R. Jack Balthazar, by Niki Delacueva; below and bottom right courtesy of Mille Fiori Floral Design, by 2me Studios

Mille Fiori Floral Design
Silky. Flutter. Fragrant.

Mille Fiori is much more than a floral design studio. Cina Park and her team open the doors to their stylish space daily, inviting veteran and up-and-coming event planners, photographers, and designers to the upstairs loft designed by Rrivre Davies of Rrivre Works. As a way of giving back to the community, Cina runs workshops detailing the basics of flower preparation, color matching, and presentation, encouraging new talent to pursue the career that has brought her so much happiness.

Photographs by Donald Norris

R. Jack Balthazar
Modern. Inspired. Enchanting.

When Rene and Niki Delacueva say they love to throw parties, they're not kidding. They are so into entertaining friends and hosting fabulous soirées that in 2001 they decided to make a career of it. With no background in flowers or events, no mentors, no training, and no real plan, the duo felt like renegades, a rebellion that has since proven to be an invaluable part of their success as R. Jack Balthazar.

Photographs: above and top right by Steven Lam; right by Tyler Boye

At the beginning, Niki and Rene may not have known the names of all the different flowers, but they knew how they wanted them to look, what feeling they wanted the blooms to evoke—the rest, they decided, could be figured out. Avoiding a formulaic approach at all costs, the married couple takes 100 percent of their inspiration from the radiant bride and how she wants to be seen on her most important day.

Photographs: above and left by Docuvitae; top left by Megan Sorel

One of the ways in which R. Jack Balthazar ensures totally unique results is through developing a story line that represents the couple's past, future, and aesthetic preferences—everyone's story is different, and everyone's floral look should be too. Whether simple or complex, relevant facets of the story find their way into the floral design as well as other visual presentations throughout the event's meticulously curated setting.

Photographs by Niki Delacueva

When it comes to cakes and invitations...

Fantasy Frostings more than lives up to its name; with plenty of cake, frosting, and filling flavors to choose from, the bakery also offers an array of small bites that create wonderland-like dessert tables. I also recommend sampling the flavors of The Butter End Cakery, Kimberly Bailey's fabulous shop that offers exquisitely baked and decorated wedding cake as well as "not cake," a category that encompasses sweet treats of all sorts, perfect as complements to a dessert table or to send home as favors. If you want your invitation to set the flavor of the event well before guests even arrive, meet branding guru Marc Friedland and his Creative Intelligence team. A Papier is another solid resource that has a great reputation for combining interesting materials, from velvet and crystals to ribbon and plastic, with finely crafted papers and beautiful printing techniques to give just the right look for any occasion. I also like the work of Copper Willow Paper Studio, which has gorgeous papers, great vintage presses, and truly talented invitation designers and calligraphers.

Photographs courtesy of Marc Friedland Couture Communications, left by Cia Canali, below by John Ellis

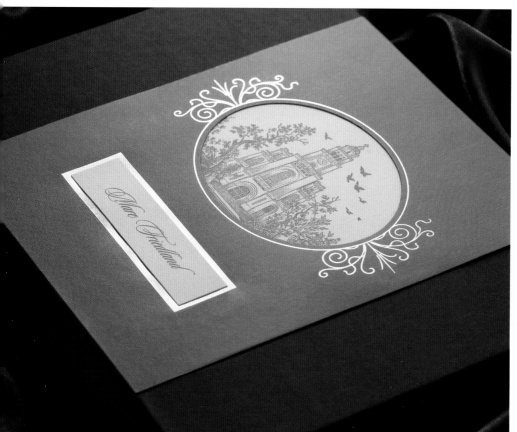

Fantasy Frostings
Goodness. Layers. Artistry.

Wouldn't it be wonderful if every planning meeting could involve dessert? Cake artist and Fantasy Frostings proprietor Leslie Maynor-Anderson likes to get to know all of her brides and event hosts over a few slices of cake so that she can help them hone in on original flavor combinations that will reflect their personal tastes. A trendsetter for more than three decades, Leslie doesn't just make chocolate cake. She bakes gourmet creations like her signature Chocolate Fudge Surprise, where the cake is layered with hand-beaten fudge, dark chocolate mousse, ganache, and crushed English toffee—decadent to be sure. For those with a taste for the lighter side of desserts, Leslie has plenty of other savory suggestions.

Photographs: above by Holly Steen; top and bottom left by Suthi Picotte

When it comes to preserving memories...

I love the work of Miki & Sonja Photography and the owners are equally wonderful; they met at the prestigious Brooks Institute of Photography and have been shooting together ever since—who better to creatively document a wedding? Joy Marie Photography is another great studio, best known for its documentary style that produces images that are "sexy and real; fine art with a touch of fashion." If you are looking for a photographer with an edge, Yvette of Yvette Roman Photography got her start by shooting stars; she's of course since made quite a name for herself by capturing romance of weddings in Palm Springs and overseas. David of David Robin Films is the consummate filmmaker, whose down-to-earth personality and artistic flair find their way into all of his work, giving it an unmistakably genuine quality. I also like the approach of Living Cinema's Curtis Heyne, who utilizes a combination of equipment: digital to ensure that every event is captured in its entirety, film to capture the raw emotion of the most important moments.

Photographs by Elizabeth Messina Photography

Photograph by Elizabeth Messina Photography

San Diego

by Thomas Bui, Thomas Bui Lifestyle

San Diego is a land of contrasts. Of course the miles and miles of gorgeous beaches that line the coast are what first come to mind—and rightfully so. But the city and its surrounding communities offer so much more than that and therefore are some of my favorite locales for a destination wedding. From lush vegetation to desert climates, high-end hotels to historic inns, vibrant urban hangouts to relaxing activities, the eighth-largest city in the U.S. stretches the imagination with its amazing ability to cater to a thousand different desires all within about an hour's drive.

When it comes to beautiful backdrops for nuptial commitments and celebrations, the Pacific Ocean is something that just can't be topped. Sparkling water, gentle breezes, dancing waves, and the warming sun naturally create this amazing romantic ambience. I really enjoy showing off the variety of coastal venues and locations that line the region's 70 miles of beaches.

Photographs: above ©iStockphoto.com/ekash; facing page ©iStockphoto.com/Alysta

175

Yet planning a wedding on this long stretch of beachfront property requires the knowledge and finesse of someone who knows the area well. For example, ceremonies on the sand require a permit, which can be obtained exactly 365 days prior to the event; for popular dates and locations, the permit is given based on a lottery system or a first-come, first-served basis. Generally, beach receptions are prohibited, although exceptions are made at Hotel del Coronado since it owns beachfront property. Also important to note is a noise curfew, which requires all outdoor receptions to conclude music by 10 p.m.

Photographs: left by Paul Barnett; below ©iStockphoto.com/ compassandcamera

Aside from oceanfront locations, San Diego has numerous other options that are just as beautiful. For a completely different atmosphere, I suggest heading east across the city where the topography varies from lush foothills and mile-high mountains to the historic mining town of Julian and the 600,000-acre Anza Borrego Desert State Park. Then there's Balboa Park, the largest urban cultural park in the U.S. with 15 museums, indoor and outdoor theaters, art galleries, gardens, and of course, the well-known San Diego Zoo. A little to the north, it's all about wide open spaces and the beauty of nature, where pristine beaches, wildlife and nature preserves, and picturesque seaside villages dot the landscape. I love the unique finds toward the south, from Whaley House Museum—known as the most haunted house in America—to Point Loma with breathtaking 360-degree views.

Photographs: above by True Wedding Photography; right ©iStockphoto.com/uschools

After we nail down the vision of the wedding, the variety of one-of-a-kind venues and professionals makes it easy for me to find just the right fit. In La Jolla, for example, Spanish-style architecture and a relaxed atmosphere evoke a sort of Mediterranean feel. Further north and inland, Rancho Bernardo is set amidst golf courses and wineries. And who could forget about Coronado, dubbed the "Crown City," reflecting seaside bliss for all. The historical ambience in Mission Valley, where the first of California's Spanish missions was founded in 1769, is unforgettable. Options at each location then create the magic, whether it's an elephant processional for a stunning addition to an Indian wedding or a helicopter ride that creates a dramatic exit for the newlyweds.

Photographs: this page by Luna Photo; facing page top by Gene Higa Photography; facing page bottom by Braja Mandala Wedding Photography

From luxurious mansions, magnificent estates, and charming inns to traditional ballrooms and waterfront penthouses, San Diego captures dozens of distinct ambiences. Paired with the area's pervasive laid-back but sophisticated energy, the region is essentially a wedding paradise.

Photographs: this page by Cene Higa Photography; facing page by James Johnson Photography

When it comes to hotels...

There is no shortage of amazing places to lay your head. In the heart of downtown, The US Grant is inimitable in its blending of historical ties and modern luxuries. At The Grand Del Mar, I notice that expectations are always blown away. And who wouldn't be impressed with its Old World elegant charm, and serene canyon preserve location. True to the property's equestrian rancho lineage, Estancia La Jolla Hotel & Spa reflects warmth through sprawling lush courtyards, clay tile roofs, and one-of-a-kind art that is interspersed amidst the campus-like setting. Just 25 minutes north of the city, The Inn at Rancho Santa Fe is hidden among the golden foothills, inspiring nature lovers and romantics alike. And it's difficult to talk of San Diego without mentioning Hotel del Coronado with its iconic red turrets and Victorian style, often heralded as one of America's best beach resorts.

Photographs courtesy of Thomas Bui Lifestyle, above by Paul Barnett Photography, top left by Aquario Studio Inc., left by Gene Higa Photography

The US Grant

Exquisite. Storied. Style.

Ideally located in downtown San Diego, The US Grant, a Luxury Collection Hotel, celebrates more than 100 years as the city's crown jewel. The hotel weaves its storied past throughout the richly appointed surroundings while offering the amenities of a modern residential palace. Sparkling crystal chandeliers, hand-loomed silk carpets, and fine art create a lavish atmosphere fit for royalty—or a President, after whom the hotel was named. Guestrooms and suites feature stunning details and plush accommodations, and ballrooms evoke an unrivaled sense of authenticity and marvel. Whether planning a weekend getaway or royal affair, the iconic hotel presents an inspiring setting steeped in legendary style.

Photographs courtesy of The US Grant

When it comes to venues...

Scripps Seaside Forum in La Jolla is the epitome of a California setting: oceanfront views and warm, contemporary architecture make for a stunning ambience. For a more urban feel, I recommend Culy Warehouse; its raw downtown space is a designer's dream, providing the perfect versatile background to create any look. If you prefer an artsy vibe, then the Museum of Contemporary Art in La Jolla—with ocean views and distinctive architectural design—or The San Diego Museum of Art—with multiple spaces, including the court and sculpture garden that overlook Balboa Park—is sure to meet your desires. And a genius idea by Jamie Ehrsam, Estate Weddings and Events partners with private estates to offer a variety of unmatched, virtually unrestricted, gorgeous venues throughout the area.

Photographs courtesy of Thomas Bui Lifestyle, above and left by Angie Silvy Photography, top left by True Photography Weddings

When it comes to catering...

The goal is to find one organization that you can completely trust to do its job—and more—to perfection. Coast Catering by Barry Layne is one such firm, where Barry's experience and dedication to pleasing the palate can hardly be topped. Waters Fine Catering is no less deserving of your complete confidence, and the focus on craftsmanship and simplicity is refreshing. At Giuseppe Restaurants & Fine Catering, my breath is constantly taken away by the exquisite details that transform any occasion from great to out of this world. With more than three decades under its belt, Crown Point Catering is an undeniably reliable resource. Founder Vicki Hamilton has nurtured a dedication and familial quality among the staff that results in tantalizing events. In a slightly different take on the traditional craft, Dining Details provides personal chefs for all occasions, boasting a passion and positive energy that only adds to the inspiring cuisine.

Photographs courtesy of Coast Catering by Barry Layne

Coast Catering by Barry Layne
Quality. Creativity. Professionalism.

Artistic and fresh with modern flair best describes culinary delights prepared by executive chef Barry Layne of Coast Catering. A successful catered affair is dependent on three things: quality, creativity, and professionalism. Coast Catering has all of these ingredients for success. With a boutique-style approach backed by numerous decades in the industry, Barry and his team make anything from an intimate brunch to a five-course luxurious gala a memorable gastronomic experience. His sincere love for pleasing people's palates—whether through classic favorites or creative cuisine—shows in every dish that's prepared, and it's one reason why his reputation for providing outstanding full-service catering services is well-known across the region.

Photographs: above by Phillip DeFalco; top right by True Photography; right by Paul Barnett

When it comes to floral design...

Isari Flower Studio + Event Design is more like an art studio than a floral shop, especially when you see owner Tam Ashworth at work creating one of her extraordinary masterpieces. And I am always amazed by everything that comes from Adorations Botanical Artistry. The team astounds me in its ability to perfectly blend the classical with the contemporary time and again. At Botanica, unbelievable designs have been flying out of the studio for more than a decade, each one reflecting the individuality of the event and carefully highlighting the features of the location. To summarize Kathy Wright & Co.'s work in one word, I would say it's distinctive. Every project boasts a classy, creative, outside-the-box style that you'll never see again. Jennifer Cole Florals is another studio I love, in particular for Jennifer's refreshingly light style that speaks of romance and elegance with every flower.

Photographs: above courtesy of Adorations Botanical Artistry, by Bobby Earle; top right and right courtesy of Isari Flower Studio + Event Design, top right by Luna Photo, right by La Vida Creations

Adorations Botanical Artistry
Imaginative. Charming. Tailored.

Vibrant colors, lush arrangements, and textural combinations are all part of the everyday atmosphere at Adorations Botanical Artistry. In a unique style that is simultaneously luxurious and approachable, Adorations brings forth lavish expressions of the soon-to-be-wedded.

Photographs: left by Luna Photo; below by Joshua Aull Photography; bottom left by Cary Pennington Photography

Isari Flower Studio + Event Design
Unprecedented. Creating. Alive.

Floral designer is appropriate but the title of artist really captures the level of finesse and beauty created by the stylists at Isari Flower Studio + Event Design. Not your average designs, these floral arrangements go way beyond what has been done before. Through changing the way they view natural materials, the artists open their eyes to the beauty and opportunity to transform the colors and shapes into living art.

Photographs: above and top by Darin Fong; top left by Paula Luna, Luna Photo; left by Tim Otto Photography

Whether they are enhancing the venue, capturing the personality of the nuptial couple, or creating an ambience, Isari's owner Tam Ashworth and her fabulous team not only inspire but also insert a little more life into the event. Extraordinary details, bold blooms, bewitching shades, and intoxicating aromas awaken the senses; the designs are simply breathtaking.

Photographs: below and bottom left by Christine Chang; right by Darin Fong; bottom right by Jo Latter

When it comes to cakes and invitations...

Sweet Cheeks Baking Co. is the place to go for local, organic, and healthful ingredients; wholesome items are sure to make it into every bite. And I can't forget about CAKE. Featured on The Food Network's "Cake Challenge," the boutique bakery creates simply stunning, delicious cakes. Then there's Michele Coulon Dessertier, where a few ingredients are transformed into edible works of art. Michele's European and culinary backgrounds influence her confectionary concoctions, prompting the use of fresh ingredients and a genuine love for desserts. In the way of invitations, it's exciting to look through the many options, but it can be overwhelming. Enter these fabulous professionals. Rock Paper Scissors Design was born from founder Rachel Baker's passion for the perfect stationery, and that enthusiasm is still going strong. Most importantly, she understands how her brides and grooms want to be treated and how important that big day really is. Jennifer Dailard is another creative genius, whose experience in advertising and design has made Simply Posh Design into a studio you must visit.

Photographs: below courtesy of Sweet Cheeks Baking Co.; top and bottom left courtesy of Rock Paper Scissors Design, top by Beautiful Day Photography, bottom by Studio Carré Photography

Sweet Cheeks Baking Co.
Heavenly. Notable. Sustainable.

At Sweet Cheeks Baking Co., goodness is baked into every bite, quite literally. The woman-owned bakery caters to those who prefer local, organic, and healthful ingredients in their confectionary treats, and offers gluten-free and vegan options that are equally yummy and beautifully designed. Through ingredients such as organic butter, flaxseed, farmer's market berries and nuts, and cage-free chicken eggs, the bakery goddesses at Sweet Cheeks have created a mouthwatering assortment of amazing cakes, cupcakes, and desserts that are both sumptuously delicious and surprisingly wholesome.

Photographs: above by Brandon Kidd Photography; top left by Carrie McCluskey Photography; left by Laura Christin Photography

Rock Paper Scissors Design
Couture. Personalized. Divine.

The sky is the limit at Rock Paper Scissors Design. Founder-designer Rachel Baker is in love with designing unique invitations and stationery personalized exclusively to each couple's vision. To begin, Rachel works closely with you to glean an understanding of your dream wedding theme. She then helps you select the highest quality materials from an infinite paper selection and palette of ink colors, along with proper wording and printing styles including letterpress, offset, thermography, engraving, foil, or embossing. Rachel is skilled at designing printed and multi-dimensional works of art using silk flowers, fine fabric, textural organic touches, and exquisite embellishments. Her couture creations will become your signature, while beckoning wedding guests with beauty and delight.

Photographs: left by Studio Carré Photography; bottom left and bottom by Beautiful Day Photography; below by creative focus photography

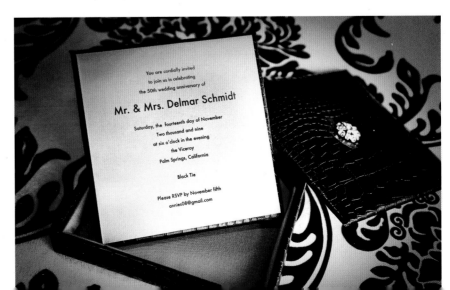

When it comes to preserving memories...

Tim Otto's talented photojournalistic approach and experience in local venues is only eclipsed by his enthusiastic, warm personality. The unparalleled setup at True Photography Weddings has always impressed me. A small, technically savvy, creative, personable team carefully culled by founder Aaron Feldman ensures that every detail is addressed and the team's refined photography vision is inherent in every project. For an unconventional approach, one of my favorites is Luna Photo; Michael and Paula's work is a fusion of documentary, fine art, fashion, and lifestyle. Known around the world for his unrehearsed photojournalistic talent—especially in a black and white medium—Paul Barnett has an uncanny ability to capture those poignant moments in a new way. Boyd Harris Photographs is another example of San Diego's best. Not only are Boyd's shots amazing, but he genuinely gets to know the family and guests so that he feels more like a friend than a hired professional.

Photographs: right and bottom right by Tim Otto Photography; below courtesy of Concepts Event Design, by Studio Castillero

Tim Otto Photography
Moments. Expression. Distinct.

A longtime interest in capturing people's individual spirit and natural expressions led Tim Otto to channel his formal graphics and photography education and commercial and portrait photography experience into his true calling: weddings. Whether he's shooting an intimate setting on the beach or a grand, elegant celebration, Tim artfully captures the natural emotions of the event through a photojournalistic style, approaching the wedding as if it were his own special day. Each dynamic image is evidence of his passion, creativity, and warm personality, which allow the photos to become more than just ink on a page; they're beautiful moments to reflect on forever.

Photographs by Tim Otto Photography

Concepts Event Design
Comprehensive. Brilliant. Create.

The creative genius behind Concepts Event Design's husband-and-wife duo of Federico and Haydee Alderete is astounding. With family at the core of their inspiration, they create the most stunning events by combining Federico's intuitive sense of design and skilled craftsmanship with Haydee's discerning eye and exquisite assortment of custom elements—fine linens, furniture, and dance floors—and other items like beautiful chandeliers.

Photographs: above by David Champagne; top right by Paul Barnett; right by Cene Higa and Braja Mandala

Their abilities and resources make for unlimited design possibilities that are characterized by elegance and class, with close attention paid even to the finest detail. The results are nothing less than absolute perfection. Every event is an exquisite blend of tasteful style and appropriate beauty, truly exhibiting their vibrancy and artistry.

Photographs: right and bottom right by Gene Higa and Braja Mandala; below by Paul Barnett

Tiffany Monday
Timeless. Chic. Gorgeous.

With a passion for creating exquisite hair designs—classic elegance and celebrity chic—Tiffany Monday beautifies brides throughout the San Diego area. Tiffany focuses on you, on location, creating a signature look to reflect your personality. To complement any hairstyle, this go-to beauty expert also offers makeup services. Tiffany transforms your hair for the reception, while giving flawless touchups all day long. A specialist in applying clip-in extensions for long, luscious locks, Tiffany treats you like a celebrity throughout your red carpet occasion. Whether you wear a traditional veil or jeweled accessories, want a demure style for day, glam tresses by night, or both looks by doing a quick hair alteration—it's all about enhancing your natural beauty so you'll be portrait-perfect.

Photographs: above left by KLK Photography; above right by Braedon Photography; top left by Studio EMP; left by John & Joseph Photography; all makeup design by Beauty by Berit

Photograph by Elizabeth Messina Photography

Santa Barbara
by Colette Lopez and Kaitlin Lopez, La Fete

When you visit Santa Barbara, you are invited to experience the city—its alluring sights, sounds, and tastes—just like the locals. You can't help but slow down from the hectic pace of daily life just to take everything in. While enjoying a freshly brewed cappuccino at a waterfront café in 70-degree weather, don't hesitate to ask a perfect stranger at the next table over for sightseeing advice. Santa Barbara is the kind of place that's too beautiful to keep all for yourself; you want everyone who visits to fall in love with it. And they do.

For its scenic aspects, like the sparkling Pacific Ocean and rugged mountain ranges, and luxurious quality of life, Santa Barbara is known as The American Riviera, "where life itself is a fine art." Towering palm trees gently sway with the ocean breeze, waves crash into the shoreline as a sensory experience, and the unmistakable salt air and orange blossoms make you aware that this paradise is in fact real. The city's unique orientation to the coastline makes the climate consistently mild, which is especially convenient for planning outdoor activities and events.

Photographs: above by BB Photography; facing page ©iStockphoto.com/DavidMSchrader

Whether bicycling along State Street with its famed Spanish Colonial-style architecture of stucco and terracotta tile roofs, walking the pier, picnicking on the beach while watching the surfers, or touring the missions or gardens, there is always something new to discover. We like to arrange multiple events surrounding the wedding—a welcome party, a bridal lunch, an excursion, a rehearsal dinner, and often a farewell brunch—so that friends and family can meet, mingle, and form relationships of their own. Between these parties and the wedding ceremony and reception, we always recommend mixing up the scenery a bit so that people have a natural tour of the region.

Photographs: above by Melissa Musgrove Photography; top left by Stephanie Hogue Photography; left by Barnaby Draper Photography

In order for people to truly get to know Santa Barbara, we encourage them to get out on the water, whether lounging on a catamaran, parasailing on a speedboat, paddle boarding, kite boarding, surfing, or sailing over to the Channel Islands. For the land-lovers, activities are equally plentiful: fun Jeep tours for the guys, relaxing spa and shopping days for the gals, chauffeured wine tastings, volleyball or golf tournaments, and historic tours of Santa Barbara sights for all. Parades, parties, markets, and festivals are held throughout the year, and integrating them into the wedding weekend's schedule of events is a great way to keep the excitement level high and set the stage for unforgettable memories.

Photographs: right ©iStockphoto.com/compassandcamera; below ©iStockphoto.com/DavidMSchrader; bottom right by Docuvitae

Our family has been blessed to live in this city for six generations, and with plenty of event planning experience, we know precisely what's required to create a unique and stylized production. To make the planning process a sheer pleasure, brides and grooms fill out a detailed questionnaire before their first visit. What's the vision: romantic winery, boutique hotel, private estate, five-star resort, garden paradise, rustic countryside, beach chic, or a family home? The diverse topography of Santa Barbara lends itself to virtually any wedding-day wish. Once we get a sense of how modern, traditional, casual, or formal the event needs to be, we plan a great itinerary showcasing all that the region has to offer. From there, we decide on the main locations and hone in on the central vision. Then we can select the right professional team and give them enough creative direction to be successful and enough freedom to produce something truly extraordinary. We ensure that everyone from invitation artist to caterer is on the same page by putting together an inspiration board of the design, color theme, and creative details that succinctly conveys the goal.

Photographs by BB Photography

While each wedding's design is as unique as the bride and groom, most people are drawn to décor that captures the natural splendor of Santa Barbara—it's what piqued their curiosity in the first place. It's no wonder that couples across the United States make this their wedding destination—and guests around the world don't hesitate to fly in for the special occasion, and perhaps a few extra days of vacationing. Whether your first visit is to marry the love of your life, to celebrate with friends and family, or simply to relax in one of the most beautiful places on earth, the magic of Santa Barbara will draw you back again and again.

Photographs: this page by Stephanie Hogue Photography; facing page top and bottom right by Docuvitae; facing page bottom left by Melissa Musgrove Photography

When it comes to hotels...

San Ysidro Ranch is sort of our claim to fame, since it regularly appears on prestigious lists of top resorts around the world; aside from that, we're partial to the personal decorative touches in each of the 41 cottages and suites and the magical quality of its grounds. Located just a block from State Street and replete with a pool deck, Canary Hotel is boutique and fabulous, outfitted with chic Moroccan furnishings and décor. Four Seasons Resort The Biltmore Santa Barbara is a good choice for out-of-town guests who already love the brand and want to feel at home but still get a taste of the local culture through the classic Spanish Colonial architecture and ocean views. For a more intimate experience steeped in history, look into the Montecito Inn, which was built in 1928 by cinema legend Charlie Chaplin—you can even borrow Chaplin's films to enjoy in-room. Bacara Resort is another great property steeped in Old Hollywood charm, and its architecture and 78 beachfront acres are the epitome of understated elegance and serenity.

Photographs courtesy of San Ysidro Ranch, by Bill Zeldis

San Ysidro Ranch
Tranquil. Romantic. Classic.

San Ysidro Ranch is quintessential Santa Barbara. Nestled in wine country and overlooking the Pacific, the hotel is where John and Jackie Kennedy honeymooned and where countless others have since chosen to reconnect with nature, themselves, and their loved ones. Whether staying in a designer bungalow-style cottage or a finely appointed ranch room, luxury is all around in true Rosewood Hotels & Resorts style. Hike or bike through the Santa Ynez Mountains, golf on coastal courses, dine with inspiring views and delectable fare, and relax with a spa treatment, at the beach, or by the pool. Every day offers a new adventure.

Photographs courtesy of San Ysidro Ranch

When it comes to venues...

It's hard to go wrong because of the region's rich history, picturesque vistas, and reputation for high-end affairs. Established in 1786 by the Spanish Franciscans, Old Mission Santa Barbara is among the city's most memorable landmarks and has been lovingly updated and preserved over the years. The 1910-established Santa Barbara Polo & Racquet Club is a great choice for the creative freedom that the expansive grounds afford—you can do tents of all sizes, drape fabric overhead to foster an open yet intimate feel, or have something indoors with fabulous architecture as the backdrop. For those looking for more of a formal garden setting, we highly recommend Lotusland, a nearly 40-acre garden nestled in a quiet neighborhood—there's a tremendous variety of themed settings, from tropical to Japanese to desert. Montecito Country Club is another notable venue because it overlooks Santa Barbara's beautiful harbor as well as the Channel Islands; it's a sister company of Four Seasons Resort The Biltmore Santa Barbara, so you already know the level of service to expect.

Photographs courtesy of Santa Barbara Polo & Racquet Club, right by Ray Anthony Photography, below and bottom right by Melissa Musgrove Photography

Santa Barbara Polo & Racquet Club
History. Tradition. Elegance.

People are initially drawn to the Santa Barbara Polo & Racquet Club for its visually stunning grounds: just a stone's throw from the beautiful Pacific Ocean with the Santa Ynez Mountains as a backdrop. Founded in 1911, it is the third-oldest operating polo club in the United States; tennis, swim, and fitness elements were incorporated in the mid 70s, so it truly has something for everyone. To host an event here, you don't even need to be a member—or be sponsored by one—and the level of service and detail attentiveness is a tradition 100 years strong.

Photographs by Ray Anthony Photography

Whether entertaining a few of your closest family and friends or having a grand affair for thousands, the Santa Barbara Polo & Racquet Club is truly a blank canvas. The club is among the most flexible venues in the region: it accepts a maximum of one wedding per week, allows advance access to vendors, and is one of the only locations in Santa Barbara County that allows entertainment beyond the standard 10 p.m. cutoff time.

Photographs by Ray Anthony Photography

The club's culinary team of Lafond's Pampered Palate specializes in customizing menus and service to suit any taste and budget. A popular place for dinner and dancing, the clubhouse is an historical building that is dedicated to celebrating the sport of polo and the importance of gathering with friends and family. The walls are adorned with polo and social photographs dating back to the early 1900s that serve as great conversation pieces. For those interested in the complete polo experience, the club offers private exhibition matches accompanied by an introduction to "the sport of kings." The tradition of divot stomping, as seen in Julia Roberts' "Pretty Woman," is a part of every match, and guests are encouraged to participate. The more adventurous may choose to take part in golf cart polo.

Photographs by Melissa Musgrove Photography

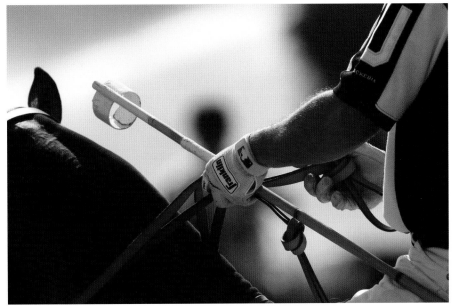

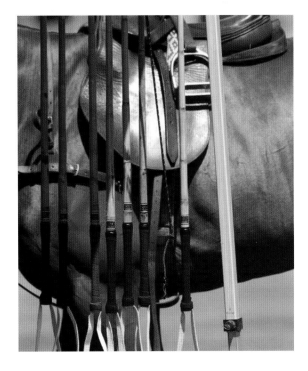

Wherever you are on the Santa Barbara Polo & Racquet Club's expansive and diverse property, you're surrounded by beauty and elegance. Hosts and photographers alike enjoy whimsical photo opportunities in the grandstands, in front of the scoreboard, or in the rustic stables, which at times contain some of the world's highest caliber thoroughbred horses. The property encompasses the best of what Mother Nature has to offer: views of the glistening Pacific Ocean and the Channel Islands, towering trees, blue skies, sunshine, and large areas of pristinely landscaped grounds.

Photographs by David Lominska

When it comes to catering...

Santa Barbara has plenty of savory options created with locally sourced, oftentimes organic ingredients. Because of the city's worldly vibe, you can find pretty much any form of ethnic cuisine you could possibly want, which is wonderful for theme continuity. Most people opt for a fusion of flavors, and the area's top culinary wizards never disappoint. Duo Catering & Events' two-pronged focus on presentation and taste often means inventing—according to the bride and groom's preferences—special dishes such as coconut lemongrass soup prepared with farm-fresh ingredients. Miranda Catering focuses on contemporary American cuisine with signatures like grilled lamb saddle with lingonberry gastrique. We love the approach of New West Catering, which sources almost exclusively from boutique farms and ranches that emphasize sustainable practices; its executive chef trained with celebrities Dean Fearing and Bobby Flay. Seasons Catering is another special company with a broad array of offerings, and the executive chef is so enthused about her art form that in addition to catering, she offers gourmet cooking classes. For unexpected combinations, also consider SBB Gourmet Catering, whose list of signatures like asparagus bisque, potato gnocchi, and smoked Texas-style beef brisket just keeps growing.

Photographs courtesy of Duo Catering & Events, by BB Photography

Duo Catering & Events
Organic. Piquant. Crafted.

Meet Ashley Transki and Brian Congdon: friends, chefs, and the founders of Duo Catering & Events, whose style emphasizes the harmonious relationship between locally grown organic produce and culinary creativity. Compressed watermelon with caviar, limes, sea salt, and lemon basil; roasted vermillion rock fish with parsley leaf, lemon, and chili flake salad; duck confit with garland chrysanthemum and preserved lemon on an apple crouton; and roasted Roots Farms beet croquet with pink peppercorn and pistachio-studded chevre are but a few of their innovative dishes.

Photographs by BB Photography

Hailing from the East Coast and having lived in a variety of locales, Ashley's culinary journey has been largely self-guided, enriched by rare opportunities to work with regional seafood and exotic meats at highly desirable establishments. A better complement could not be found than in Brian, whose natural proclivity for cooking became evident at age six and proved unstoppable by the time he attended the California Culinary Academy. The chefs' individual and shared pursuits of food and flavor have been realized in Southern California, where there's a bounty of natural inspiration, fresh ingredients, and an adventurous clientele.

Photographs by BB Photography

When it comes to floral design...

Remember that Southern California has a delightfully subtropical climate, so lots of different types of flowers are readily available to help you carry the theme of your event from start to finish. We really connect with the organic feel of Mindy Rice Floral's designs, which are usually complemented by hand-sewn linens, costumed design elements, and other special touches—Mindy is high energy, high enthusiasm all the time, so it's really refreshing to collaborate with her. The event design and floral studio of R. Jack Balthazar is all about experiencing life with all of the senses, and the floral experts truly elevate their craft to an art form that is entirely necessary to establish the right ambience. Santa Barbara Style has a reputation for classic, romantic floral décor that often incorporates trees, draped fabric, and unexpected props. The mastermind behind Cody Floral Design is Laura Sangas, who feels that each wedding is like a painting, the bride is the artist, and it's the privilege of the florist to pull together seemingly unrelated wishes into a beautiful composition that expresses the event's theme. For a floral design experience that has a distinct Southern California vibe, stop by SR Hogue's charming studio, where even the most traditional and timeless designs feel innovative and fresh.

Photographs courtesy of R. Jack Balthazar, above and right by Amy & Stuart Photography, top right by Elizabeth Messina Photography

R. Jack Balthazar
Dreamy. Organic. Residential.

A love for all things glamorous and unique helps Niki and Rene Delacueva funnel their passion into wholly original floral designs. Branches, grasses, fun leaves and foliage, trees, succulents, fancy ribbons, crystals, and feathers all feature heavily in their work, but it's not unheard of for a vintage vessel, family treasure, or time-worn memento to be woven into the mix.

Photographs by Amy & Stuart Photography

With style and personality to spare, the leaders of R. Jack Balthazar are just as at home in big open spaces as they are in innovatively designed small places. Themes are not a constricting obstacle but rather a directive challenge, an opportunity to push their creative boundaries and discover never-before-seen ways to display flowers and other materials to their best advantage.

Photographs: below by Niki Delacueva; right and bottom right by Elizabeth Messina Photography; facing page by Amy & Stuart Photography

When it comes to cakes and invitations...

Laura Hooper Calligraphy does simply beautiful work for invitations and other printed materials; we love that the owner is involved in the conceptualization of every project and likes to personally calligraphy or letter the materials when possible. Lazaro Press is another great resource, specializing in letterpress and offset printed pieces. In the way of dessert, Sweet and Saucy Shop is as fun and original as its name implies; the bakery prepares the full range of sweets and is run by confection chefs, lollipop experts, sugar flower specialists, and cake artists. Most known for its tiered wedding cakes accented with originals like Kahlúa mousse or passion fruit curd, Christine Dahl Pastries also offers petits fours and other tasty treats. Enjoy Cupcakes specializes in everyone's favorite personal-sized confection in extraordinary flavors like chocolate blackberry syrah, pomegranate mango chardonnay, and maple macadamia nut, no doubt evocative of our proximity to wine country.

Photographs courtesy of Laura Hooper Calligraphy, above by Steve Steinhardt Photography, left by Mi Belle Photography

Laura Hooper Calligraphy
Paper. Delightful. Letters.

Nothing says romance like the personal touch of an invitation or menu created by hand—designed and lettered to reflect the style and theme of the occasion. Especially in the hyper-speed, digital world in which we live do people really appreciate the tangible, artful quality of Laura Hooper Calligraphy's work. Everyone in the wedding industry knows that a well-done invitation is the best way to ensure high attendance and set the ambience even before guests arrive, and going hand-crafted is the ultimate option.

Photographs by Steve Steinhardt Photography

Though her company is based in Southern California, Laura has contributed her signature elegance to weddings and other special occasions around the globe—yes, she's that good. From save-the-dates and formal invitations to placecards, table numbers, maps, monograms, and anything else that establishes the bride and groom's new identity together, Laura and her team are happy to lend their creative flair. Sustainable design is a huge focus, with recycled and cotton papers, reusable objects, and soy inks making regular appearances throughout their portfolio.

Photographs by Steve Steinhardt Photography

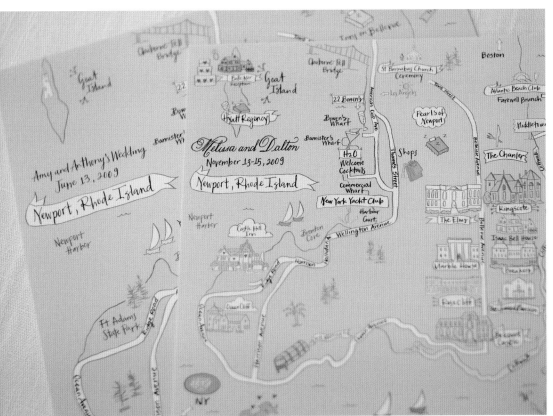

Most people tend to think of calligraphy in classical terms—the term is, after all, a derivative of the Greek words for "beautiful writing"—but in fact it is a technique that can span the whole spectrum of lettering looks. Laura Hooper Calligraphy offers more than two dozen lettering varieties, from over-the-top to totally streamlined, and the custom stationer is always inventing new looks for traditionalists, modernists, and even those who can't quite pinpoint their tastes.

Photographs by Steve Steinhardt Photography

227

When it comes to preserving memories...

We're blessed with a number of locally based, wildly talented creative types. We can help brides figure out who's right for their occasion based on whether they want a photojournalistic approach, need a whole bunch of studio-quality family portraits shot the day of the wedding, or have something else in mind. Melissa Musgrove really has a knack for seeing potential shots even before they happen in order to capture raw emotion. Stephanie Hogue lends her photographs a wonderfully romantic, almost nostalgic look—seeing the world through her lens is truly inspiring. The husband-wife team of Brian and Brady Charrette form BB Photography, which is known for documenting all aspects of the day and then editing the images into a meaningful collection that conveys not just happenings but emotions as well. For those seeking a black and white photojournalistic look, we recommend Paul Barnett's studio Barnett Photographics, which specializes in the spontaneous. Jose Villa takes a different approach, infusing a bit of creative direction to ensure that everyone looks like a star and the angles are conducive to his vision of fine art portraiture.

Photographs: left by Stephanie Hogue Photography, below by Melissa Musgrove Photography, bottom left by BB Photography

BB Photography
Energy. Perspective. Love.

As a couple passionate about their craft, photographers Brian and Brady Charrette intimately understand the roller coaster of emotions associated with weddings and are willing to do whatever it takes to fully document the special day. Their energy is of a warm, true, and honest nature, which allows them to connect with their couples and create images full of emotion and life. They truly love tapping into people's souls and it shows in every frame that bears their name.

Photographs by BB Photography

Melissa Musgrove Photography
Style. Finesse. Warmth.

Known for her ability to artistically capture everything from quiet moments to grand celebrations, Melissa Musgrove is warm, friendly, and immediately puts people at ease so they feel and look their best. Having photographed hundreds of weddings, Melissa possesses valuable experience and tremendous intuition, yet she is never content to take an ordinary approach—each couple, each event, deserves a fresh perspective. At once classic and current, Melissa's photographs are expressive works of art that convey the beauty of each moment.

Photographs by Melissa Musgrove Photography

Stephanie Hogue Photography
Classic. Timeless. Unique.

Like so many who come to sunny Southern California for school, work, or pleasure, Stephanie Hogue decided to stay. A graduate of the prestigious Brooks Institute of Photography, Stephanie is commissioned for everything from fine portraiture to wedding day festivities to national political campaigns and loves every minute of it. Because she immerses herself in so many different situations, she has a keen eye for interesting angles, which allows her to eloquently and artfully document meaningful moments to be treasured.

Photographs by Stephanie Hogue Photography

Ambient Event Design
Tasteful. Elegant. Creative.

Every event planner needs an experienced company for all of the details that make a party really special and totally seamless. Ambient Event Design is a rare blend of these creative talents. The company's highest objective is to match the host's unique vision with a distinct, flawlessly presented environment. Utilizing lighting design, fabric textures, floral expressions, technical expertise, creativity, and ingenuity, the team translates ideas and inspirations into nostalgic atmospheres that linger in memories and photographs.

Photographs by Geoff Mognis

Bella Vista Designs
Intriguing. Complete. Thoughtful.

Bella Vista Designs is an innovative lighting and design company that works throughout Southern California on private, social, and corporate functions. Combining conventional and imaginative treatments, its professional designers and technicians create ambience through custom lighting, décor, audio, and video. To determine the desired look and feel for each function, team members work closely with event hosts and sponsors throughout the creative process to develop and fine tune every detail. Careful attention is placed on creating a balanced and dynamic relationship between visual and technical components, which results in unforgettable events and lasting memories.

Photographs by Trevor Zellet

Opal Restaurant and Bar
Global. Local. Signature.

Inspire your taste buds with contemporary cuisine prepared with produce from local farms, seafood caught by local fishermen, and interesting spices from around the world. Whether it's the lemongrass-crusted fresh salmon filet with a Thai curry sauce, the herb-grilled filet mignon with a port wine and wild mushroom-Marsala cream sauce, or another magical concoction, you can expect phenomenal flavor at Opal Restaurant and Bar.

Photographs by Melissa Musgrove Photography

While retaining its status as an archetypal Santa Barbara restaurant, the 1980s-established bistro has grown in size and fame over the years. Never content to rest on its laurels, Opal features a full bar with creative contemporary cocktails and a *Wine Spectator* award-winning wine list and continues to forge ahead with cutting-edge innovations that keep it fresh, lively, and stylish.

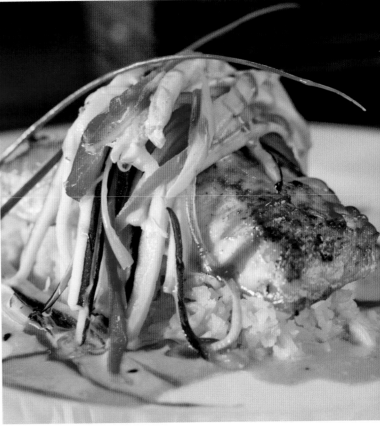

Possessing a distinctly elegant and sophisticated yet comfortable and friendly ambience—furthered by fresh floral designs by Kaleidoscope Flowers—Opal is lovingly run by Tina Takaya and Richard Yates. They insist on keeping the food exciting so their guests can experience a world of flavors all in one beautiful setting. Spanish, French, Italian, Pacific Rim, Mexican, Caribbean, Indian, Asian, and American traditions are celebrated both individually and as brilliant fusions.

Photographs by Melissa Musgrove Photography

Petros
Ambience. Tasty. Hellenic.

The same unique experience Petros Benekos brought to his
Manhattan Beach and Los Olivos restaurants is now on State
Street in Santa Barbara. Everything from the chic ambience
and European aura to the same delicious menu brings tourist
and locals alike to see what the commotion is all about.
Signature drinks and dishes like the octopus calamari and
the loukouma, a divine dessert of baby Creek doughnuts and
homemade vanilla ice cream drizzled with honey, cinnamon,
and toasted walnuts, help create the perfect setting for
unforgettable events, such as rehearsal dinners, wedding
receptions, and bridal showers.

Photographs by Cameron Ingalls Photography

Santa Monica

by Lisa Gorjestani, Details Event Planning

The city of Santa Monica is a beachside paradise that's almost too good to be true. You'll find fantastic restaurants, great shopping, attractive beaches, and a rich history all in one place. Averaging 310 days of sunshine a year, Santa Monica's sun-kissed Mediterranean climate bolsters brides' confidence in planning an outdoor ceremony. And the scenery is to die for: the city simply overflows with beaches, mountains, and other feats of nature. Despite all that, it's still incredibly accessible—there's virtually no sacrifice in convenience. No surprise here that it's a top wedding destination!

Santa Monica's history with hospitality dates back to 1885 when the first hotel was built; the city has had years to hone its talents and develop world-class accommodations worthy of their beautiful setting. From boutique to historic, modern to ultra-luxury, Santa Monica's dozens of lodging options represent something for everyone. No matter the neighborhood—downtown and Third Street Promenade, Main Street, Montana Avenue, mid-city, Ocean Park Boulevard, Pico Boulevard, or beachfront Ocean Avenue and the Santa Monica Pier—you'll experience an unforgettable stay. Many of the hotels, naturally, double as fantastic wedding venues too.

Photographs: above ©iStockphoto.com/compassandcamera; facing page ©iStockphoto.com/raisbeckfoto

239

On par with Santa Monica's scenery, climate, and luxury hotel options are the shopping and dining experiences that await. Each neighborhood of the city has its own flavor and character, from upscale to eclectic to modern to laidback. Days spent lazily browsing the shops and eating some delicious meals of any cuisine type are infinitely relaxing and a lot of fun. The restaurants make great rehearsal dinner venues, and the easily walkable and convenient destinations make Santa Monica even more of a draw for your guests.

Photographs by Elizabeth Messina Photography

The city is full of landmarks and attractions to occupy all ages and personalities. From the Looff Hippodrome carousel—a National Historic Landmark—on the 1909-built Santa Monica Pier to the La Monica Ballroom, Civic Auditorium, Santa Monica Museum of Art, and dozens of movie theaters that hearken back to the golden age of cinema, there's a wealth of things to do. Take a walk in Palisades Park for a spectacular ocean view—don't forget to check out the camera obscura—or climb the Santa Monica Steps for a good workout. Further adding to the appeal, the city is environmentally conscious: in addition to farmer's markets and community gardens, public buildings use renewable energy and public vehicles run on alternative fuel.

Photographs: left and bottom right by Yvette Roman Photography; below ©iStockphoto.com/konnithebrat

I love leading a design team to create gorgeous weddings that play to the strengths of this stunning city. We're naturals at navigating the overwhelming mass of options that result from any engagement; we streamline each couple's wants and needs into one beautiful day. My idea of the perfect wedding weekend involves a kickoff dinner followed by a dessert and cocktail reception for out-of-town guests, one exquisite wedding day, and brunch on the beach the morning after. In Santa Monica, we can set up umbrellas and chairs on the beach for a truly Southern California casual meal to close out a blissful seaside wedding weekend.

Photographs by Elizabeth Messina Photography

No matter how many weddings my team and I have done, we know that each one will be original and have its own style thanks to all of the thoughtful details that personalize the affair. The key is to be patient, unruffled, prepared, and calm—I've found that when I'm having fun and enjoying the process, my brides do too. And when the couple is relaxed, so are the guests; they rely on me to set the tone.

Photographs by Elizabeth Messina Photography

Above all, I'm thrilled to be doing exactly what I love, and I bring that passion to my weddings. I've looked out at the dance floor during the reception and caught a glimpse of the bride there with the biggest smile, unmistakable tears of joy streaming down her face—it's those moments that make it all worth it and tell me that I'm helping to create everlasting memories.

Photographs by Isabel Lawrence Photographers

245

When it comes to hotels...

Shutters on the Beach is perfect if you're looking for a haven for total relaxation; it offers a complete package in terms of ocean views, fabulous wine and food, excellent massages, and comfy accommodations for a great night's sleep. For a more active atmosphere, consider Casa del Mar, which is every bit as luxurious but also offers live music and activities that are great for large groups to mingle. Viceroy Santa Monica has quite a few claims to fame but two of my favorite aspects are the poolside cabanas and the holistic eco-luxury spa. An urban beachfront property, Shore Hotel is the area's first newly constructed LEED-certified building; it spares nothing in terms of comfort or luxury and is just a few steps from the Santa Monica Pier and Third Street Promenade. If a chic contemporary setting is where you feel most at home, The Huntley delivers that and more with fabulous interior designs mixing rich materials, textures, and motifs to create a really enveloping setting.

Photographs courtesy of Viceroy Santa Monica, by Christian Horan Photography

Viceroy Santa Monica
Sophistication. Seaside. Contemporary.

Luxurious boutique hotels are a rare find, especially when steps away from one of the most famous Pacific Coast beaches with its frothy waves, lively pier, and boardwalk. The über chic Viceroy Santa Monica stands apart as a sophisticated respite, with its coveted ocean-view suite and contemporary accommodations that rival royal suites anywhere in the world. Superlative service, designer furnishings, lavish bathrooms, feather duvets, and in-room services from the holistic GreenBliss Eco Spa make your stay at the Viceroy unforgettable. You may even want to host your reception, rehearsal dinner, or post-wedding brunch at this seaside landmark.

Photographs by Christian Horan Photography

Imagine dining alfresco at the Viceroy's Whist Restaurant seated in white wingback chairs, receiving impeccable service while savoring world-class Mediterranean cuisine prepared by executive chef Tony DiSalvo. Designed by Kelly Wearstler, its crisp contemporary lines and indoor-outdoor atmosphere provide a culinary experience that is extraordinary in every way. Enjoy a refreshing signature drink at the retro-glam Cameo Bar to relax those pre-wedding jitters. By daylight or evening candlelight, European-inspired poolside cabanas keep your romantic moments under wraps in an intimate atmosphere. And a leisurely beach stroll starts right out your door—what more could you ask for?

Photographs: above by William Innes Photography; top left by Jen O'Sullivan; left by Christian Horan Photography

When it comes to venues...

Santa Monica's most prestigious are steeped in history, which is wonderfully symbolic for a wedding, where two people's history is just beginning. Bel-Air Bay Club has been a hub of social activity since it was established back in the '20s and with a variety of indoor and outdoor event settings, it still has a magical quality. Annenberg Community Beach House was also developed during the '20s but as a vast private estate with beautifully manicured grounds—five acres of exquisite oceanfront property. With a wonderful dedication to the earth—the most historic of all elements—Tiato presents a beautiful space of reclaimed wood, recycled tiles, eco-fabrics, and recycled glass platters, both inside and on its fresh herb and citrus garden patio.

Photographs courtesy of Tiato—Kitchen Bar Garden Venue; top by Alex Vasilescu; above and left by Jimmy Cohrssen

When it comes to catering...

So much is possible. Family-owned An Catering is a Southern California institution, with the fabulous restaurant Tiato and catering facilities right here in Santa Monica. I also like Jackson Somerset's approach, which focuses on not just fine ingredients for the meal, but also considers when, where, how, and with what wine the cuisine is served. Santa Monica chefs blend top-notch training with an ingrained appreciation of coastal cuisine and lifestyle to create fabulously unique menus. The Kitchen for Exploring Foods has a great story to match its tasty fare: proprietor Peggy Dark started her career teaching cooking classes and by popular demand segued into international cooking tours and large-scale catering. Schaffer's Genuine Foods is owned by a wonderful husband and wife who dish up the most exquisite foods with a nod to local growers' organic fare. Having trained under some of Europe's top chefs and worked for some of the top catering companies in the country, they have the experience to make your event as beautiful to the eye as it is to taste.

Photographs courtesy of An Catering, right by Jessica Boone, below by Zen Todd, bottom right by Eric Raptosh

An Catering
Imaginary. Visionary. Fusion.

Crowned as "the mother of fusion cuisine" by the *San Francisco Chronicle*, executive chef Helene An heads the culinary powerhouse An Catering alongside her daughter, Catherine. Together they have created a fresh and innovative global menu that is not only custom-tailored to each host's wishes, but also fuses all the unique personalities of House of An's premier restaurants. Their eclectic brand of Euro-Vietnamese cuisine led to the An family's induction into the Smithsonian Institute. As of today, House of An boasts Crustacean Beverly Hills, AnQi in Orange County, and Tiato, its own exclusive indoor and outdoor 11,000-square-foot venue in Santa Monica with an outdoor herb garden.

Photographs: above by Mario Sanchez; right by Alex Vasilescu

Heralded as "the caterer to the stars" by the *Los Angeles Times*, An Catering has already become a household name and regularly makes appearances at Hollywood parties, upscale charity events, and intimate lavish weddings. With in-house designers and mixologists, the caterer creates memorable experiences through flawless execution. The blend of Helene's refined, Eastern-influenced holistic flavors and Catherine's unwavering standard of excellence has made An Catering ubiquitous in Southern California.

Photographs by Alex Vasilescu

When it comes to floral design...

There's a wealth of gorgeous choices. Empty Vase creates legendary bouquets, arrangements, and downright stunning topiaries that it delivers all over the city. The Hidden Garden makes use of unconventional textures and materials of the highest quality to forge creations worthy of movie premieres, magazine cover stories, and, of course, gorgeous weddings. And Mille Fiori Floral Design truly seems to have thousands of flowers' worth of creative, expertly selected designs. Jennifer McCarigle of Floral Art is our region's resident celebrity floral designer, who has shown off her star-studded designs for countless television programs and design publications. Eric Buterbaugh is another resource whose client list reads like a who's who in Hollywood and abroad. His background at Versace and Valentino in Milan have certainly influenced his sense of style, leading to designs that have been eloquently described as "opulent flowers presented in a modern way." To marry in Santa Monica means lovely, dreamy florals are an absolute must!

Photographs courtesy of Empty Vase

Empty Vase
Bright. Distinctive. Statement.

West Hollywood's Empty Vase delivers stunning and unique floral creations for hundreds of Santa Monica-based weddings, many of which include celebrity guests. Founder and floral designer Saeed Babaeean leads a diverse team capable of handling any demand with creativity and care. Each of their exquisite designs is specially tailored for the color, theme, and style of the occasion.

Empty Vase's specialties also include products not found at the typical floral studio. Animal and geometric topiaries are sure to stand out, as are lush potted orchid arrangements, sculpted to perfection and ready to be whisked to tabletops as lovely centerpieces.

In addition to their floral design services, the Empty Vase team offers full-scale event design and production, including floorplans, fabric draping, lighting, and rentals. Encouraging people to freely share their emotions and design preferences, they walk each bride through all of the elements needed to make the special day breathtaking and extraordinary.

Photographs courtesy of Empty Vase

255

The Hidden Garden
Delicate. Sophisticated. Lush.

Utilizing the highest quality products, nontraditional textures, and unique elements, the floral designers at The Hidden Garden create breathtaking arrangements for weddings of all styles, modern and classic, indoors and out, grand or simply elegant. They have designed for such big-name magazines as *People*, *Inside Weddings*, and *InStyle Weddings*, as well as for award shows, movie premieres, and launch parties, so it's no surprise that brides often feel like they're starring in their own film or walking the red carpet when they walk down the aisle.

Photographs: left by Susan Bordelon Photography; below by David Michael Photography; bottom left by Jennifer Dery

Mille Fiori Floral Design
Luminous. Exquisite. Petal.

At their very core—or stem, if you will—flowers speak a different language, touching heart and soul with their beauty. Mille Fiori Floral Design speaks that language with creations that combine exciting new ideas with timeless splendor. A dynamic mix of professional floral designers and interns in their mentor program ensures that each centerpiece, bouquet, or item of décor will benefit from a multitude of unique perspectives.

Photographs: above left and right by Steven Lam Photography; left by Aaron Delesie

When it comes to cakes and invitations...

You can't go wrong with Vanilla Bake Shop, a Santa Monica favorite with the mission of baking tasty treats from scratch with love—it's appropriately owned by a husband and wife team. The Butter End Cakery is known for creating desserts in styles ranging from entirely elegant to a little bit racy, all in good taste of course; the pastry chefs can even whip up vegan and gluten-free treats if the occasion requires. And while Fantasy Frostings certainly has a reputation for delicious wedding cakes, it also offers fabulous dessert tables filled with bite-sized morsels to replace or complement the traditional spread. In the way of invitations, Sugar Paper is one of those beautiful little shops where the minute you walk in, it is immediately clear why the shop is renowned for its design aesthetic, unparalleled taste, and perfectionism. Its designers are true ambassadors to the simple elegance of letterpress and social stationery. Susan Lee and her creative team at Papel Paper & Press produce exquisite letterpress and embossed invitations. I love how Susan's talent as a graphic artist really shines through as she helps create one-of-a-kind invitations that leave a lasting impression. Cakes and invitations dreamed up in Santa Monica are absolute showstoppers.

Photographs courtesy of Vanilla Bake Shop: right by Jason Herring Photography; below by John Solano Photography

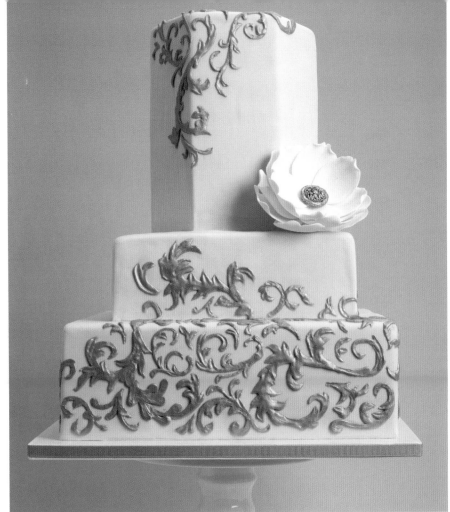

Vanilla Bake Shop
Crave. Delectable. Concoctions.

Named after the most universally beloved flavor, Vanilla Bake Shop is a Santa Monica neighborhood hotspot. Married couple Amy and Jeremy Berman established the charming bakery with the goal of making delicious desserts from scratch with contemporary design and timeless taste. Amy's mother inspired her true dedication to baking tasty treats from scratch with love. This, paired with honed expertise in catering private events and numerous accolades, makes Vanilla Bake Shop an inspired choice as a wedding baker. Quality ingredients—including Nielson Massey vanilla beans and Cuittard chocolate—lead to some of the most sought-after and craved cakes, cupcakes, and dainty sweets. Creative, sophisticated, and above all delectable, the cakes by Vanilla Bake Shop are some of the best in town.

Photographs: above by Jason Herring Photography; top left by Elizabeth Messina Photography; left by Duke Photography

When it comes to preserving memories...

Elizabeth Messina is a great resource not only because of her natural talent but also because you can just tell how much love and care she contributes to every portrait session and special occasion. Owned by a husband and wife team, Amy & Stuart Photography takes a unique approach; rather than staging the memories, they immerse themselves in their setting and patiently wait for magical moments to unfold. Yvette Roman is one of those photographers who emotes joy the minute you meet her. Her absolute love of life and wonderment at all things big and small make her a most exceptional photographer— she can always spot the one tiny detail that makes the picture perfect. If you're looking for a name with international resonance, be sure to investigate Southern California's own Joe Buissink, whose portfolio reads like Hollywood's A-List. In the world of cinematography, I'm a fan of Reel Life Pictures' ability to capture great video footage along with crisp still images and then edit everything to convey the raw emotions and heartfelt moments of the event.

Photographs by Elizabeth Messina Photography

Lighten Up
Production. Glowing. Multihued.

One element you'll never regret splurging on at your wedding is lighting. Great lighting transforms the party atmosphere and creates an unforgettable experience. Lighten Up is a Southern California lighting authority that has illuminated events since 1998. Skilled technicians deliver professional lighting on any scale, whether table pin spots, spotlights on the cake, or dance floor mood lighting. From lanterns to gobos, Lighten Up possesses the full range of lighting capabilities to create the ambience of your dreams.

Photographs courtesy of Lighten Up, Inc.

Resource One Inc.
Hues. Luxury. Creative.

Almost like magic, the color and texture of your table linens instantly defines the mood of your dinner reception or cocktail hour. That's where Roberta Karsch of Resource One Inc. steps in to give you expert advice on how to reflect your wedding theme and create a romantic ambience through a tailored blend of luxury linens, decorative accessories, and sleek ghost chairs. With more than 20 years of experience, Roberta and her team guide you in the selection process, choosing color schemes, textural effects, and elegant chair treatments to make your event a creative expression of who you are.

Photographs: above by Ron Manville Photography; left by Mike Colón Photographers

Town & Country Event Rentals
Professional. One-stop. Attentive.

With more to offer than the typical rental company, Town & Country Event Rentals prides itself on its outstanding collection of exquisite and unique furnishings for the Southern California bride. Town & Country carries a selection of more than 40 colors and styles of chairs, 18 china patterns, 20 designs of glasses and stemware, as well as an inventory of over 4,500 pieces of furniture in almost 20 different styles. Furniture selections range from ultra-contemporary to its exclusive "In the Vineyard" line of cottage-chic furnishings that encompass over 200 vintage items includes dining canopies, tables, chairs, garden swings, china, glassware, and linens.

Photographs: right and below by Tom Hinckley, Studio 1501 Inc; bottom right by Jennifer Perez

Owner and industry veteran Richard LoCuercio focuses his passion on two main principles: excellent service provided by talented professionals who really care and an unsurpassed quality and selection of furnishings that are second to none. Richard calls his clientele "the artists," and adds that he and his team are their "palette of colors and textures." Richard is always searching for new trends, traveling far and wide to tradeshows as distant as China and Europe, constantly expanding his repertoire of inventory and sourcing one-of-a-kind items that don't look like rentals. In addition to the distinct and the hard to find, Town & Country's 125,000-square-foot facility stocks a comprehensive selection of beautiful tents, lighting, dance floors, and much more, all of it cared for and maintained by the best in the business.

Photographs: above by Cold Wong Photography; right by Callaway Cable; facing page by Tom Hinckley, Studio 1501 Inc.

Santa Ynez Valley
by Rebecca Stone, Duet Weddings

Rustic charm and contemporary elegance are woven together in the Santa Ynez Valley for an unbelievable atmosphere. You'd think these qualities would contradict each other, but somehow the locals have pulled it off. Perhaps it's because of their respect for revered traditions while they continue to move forward, embracing new trends and experiences. Or maybe the blend of rural ambience with modern luxury comes from the variety of cultures that have made the area home throughout the last few centuries. Whatever the reason, the valley of rolling hills and rows of grapes begs you to host your celebration here.

Neatly tucked between the Santa Ynez Mountains and the San Rafael Mountains, and just 30 minutes north of Santa Barbara, the valley is named after the 1804 Old Mission Santa Inés, the first Spanish settlement in the area, and includes six quaint towns: Ballard, Buellton, Los Alamos, Los Olivos, Santa Ynez, and Solvang. Long before the Spanish explorers arrived in 1769, though, the Chumash Indians had a well-established community. Later, farmers and ranchers who began migrating west as early as 1850 developed a variety of industries, including cattle, sheep, olives, peaches, walnuts, prunes, apples, cherries, and quinces. A stagecoach stop in the towns of Ballard and Los Olivos—now turned into Mattei's Tavern—helped spur the region's growth.

Photographs ©iStockphoto.com/compassandcamera

Of course the real draw today is the profusion of wineries that have been established within the last few decades as vintners take advantage of the cool ocean breezes that sweep across the undulating fields. Award-winning varietals are spread across more than 75 world-class wineries and tasting rooms within the region, abundantly satisfying both the wine connoisseur and the novice drinker.

Photographs by Jose Villa

The year-round pleasant weather, gorgeous scenery, and cultural focus mean a variety of activities are available to satisfy nearly every type of personality. And, best of all, the proximity between locations is perfect for a destination wedding celebration that lasts the entire weekend—or all week as I would prefer. With a more intimate group, I suggest you start the weekend with winery tours via old-fashioned buses on a Friday evening—complete with gourmet hors d'oeuvres, of course; a larger group might be more conducive to a champagne reception at a winery or a Santa Maria-style barbecue in an open field as the sun sets. The Saturday ceremony and reception have so many options, from a formal affair to a relaxed celebration, an elegant tasting room ambience to an organic field-of-wildflowers atmosphere.

Photographs by Jose Villa

The key is to be prepared, especially for outdoor locations. The coastal breezes that are so good for the grapes can wreak havoc on escort cards, signs, menus, and floral arrangements, so be sure everything is either securely fastened or is heavy enough to withstand the wind. Also, since nights can get chilly, one of my favorite options is to create little lounge vignettes with cozy blankets, firepits, and shawls for the women. On Sunday, a lovely outdoor brunch featuring local ingredients can top off the full weekend experience.

Photographs by Jose Villa

You can also pluck apples and berries at local farms for delicious sampling, tour a lavender farm or miniature horse or donkey ranch, picnic by the water or do a bit of fishing at Cachuma Lake or Johoqui Falls, golf on a number of excellent courses, and bike and hike the stunning countryside. Boutique shopping, browsing art galleries, and antique store excursions would be perfect after a bridal luncheon, or gaming and live entertainment at Chumash Casino Resort would make a fabulous guys' night out. And if you're looking for a European experience without the need for a passport, the Danish village of Solvang is a favorite of mine, where cobblestone streets, windmills, Danish specialties like œbleskiver—a pancake-like pastry in the shape of a ball—and architecture straight from Denmark truly transport you away from everything.

Photographs by Corbin Curkin

271

In spite of all there is to do and see, my favorite thing about the Santa Ynez Valley is its ability to generate such a sense of togetherness. The small towns and quaint hotels mean that when you're not participating in group activities, you are still likely to run into friends and family on the sidewalk, which lends a very special feel. I first fell in love with the region during weekends spent here with my future husband; when we got engaged, we knew this needed to be our wedding location. Months spent researching only enhanced my love for Santa Ynez. Its romantic elegance is so natural—not contrived; that's the essence of the valley.

Photographs by Corbin Curkin

When it comes to hotels...

Fess Parker Wine Country Inn & Spa is one of my favorites; it's in a great location surrounded by fabulous restaurants and art studios, and the staff is very attentive. More traditionally speaking, Santa Ynez Inn is my choice du jour for its ornate, romantic ambience amidst opulent furnishings in a beautiful Victorian-style building. The Alisal Guest Ranch and Resort has been a luxurious hideaway with an Old West feel for generations; you couldn't ask for more romance and majesty. Upbeat and modern, Hotel Corque has plenty of rooms to accommodate large groups; as a bonus, located on-site is notable chef Bradley Ogden's fantastic bar and restaurant, where dishes like the blue cheese soufflé and tasting spoons of the house-made ice cream are must-haves. As a cozy bed and breakfast, The Ballard Inn evokes a level of comfort equivalent to home within a stylish, gorgeous country setting.

Photographs courtesy of Santa Ynez Inn, by Serena & Jason Photography

Alisal Guest Ranch and Resort
History. Pure. Distinguished.

Welcome to land unspoiled by urban crawl, where time seems reluctant to move forward. Set on a 10,000-acre working cattle ranch where horses and cattle roam on grass-covered hills that have hardly changed since the days of the Spanish vaquero, the Alisal Guest Ranch and Resort blends the best of nature with the utmost in Western-flavored hospitality.

Photographs by Trent Buckle, ProImage

Whether staying in a studio or a one-bedroom suite, a plethora of activities will certainly draw you out of the room, from golf and horseback riding to a massage or yoga class in the Alisal Guest Ranch and Resort's 6,000-square-foot fitness center and spa.

Photographs courtesy of Alisal Guest Ranch and Resort

Fess Parker Wine Country Inn & Spa
Luxury. Elegance. Legendary.

Fess Parker Wine Country Inn & Spa is a sophisticated escape with beautifully designed rooms, each featuring a warm, inviting fireplace and artwork of the local, natural surroundings. Guests come to relax and rejuvenate in an atmosphere of casual elegance and to enjoy the peacefulness of the scenic Santa Ynez Valley on California's Central Coast. The inn has a full-service spa, highly acclaimed dining, nearby signature golf courses, horseback riding, and many other recreational activities. A multitude of wine tasting rooms—including four owned by the Parker family—are just a short walk from the inn, a luxurious yet quaint retreat that offers the amenities of a larger resort.

Photographs: right and bottom right by Elizabeth Witt Photography; below courtesy of Petros

Santa Ynez Inn
Striking. Unforgettable. Fulfill.

A wedding calls for romance and luxury amidst beautiful surroundings. That's exactly what Santa Ynez Inn delivers. Its Victorian charm, modern amenities, and stylish venue spaces—including a beautiful lawn and gardens—offer an elegant, tranquil atmosphere amidst the stunning Santa Barbara wine country and breathtaking mountains. The warm hospitality of the staff makes all the difference, too. With a sumptuous gourmet breakfast, evening wine and hors d'oeuvres, and nightly desserts that are all included in a stay at the inn, what more could you ask for?

Photographs: above and left by Serena & Jason Photography; top left by Linda Chaja Photography

When it comes to venues...

Cainey Vineyard is the quintessential wine country setting: a lovely lawn and quaint tasting room are gently embraced by rows of grapes and old oak trees. A newer venue but no less alluring, Demetria Estate's sprawling patio has a canopy of towering grand trees with Old World architecture, gorgeous landscaping, and lovely grapevines all around. For the best of both worlds—gorgeous landscape views and the comfort and luxury of an indoor location—Petros is certainly on my list. At Zaca Creek Ranch, a working cattle ranch steeped in the traditions of Old California, the delightful barn residence maintains a sort of cowboy charm while still being luxurious. Transporting guests back to early Americana while still enjoying modern conveniences, Figueroa Mountain Farmhouse is a secluded, charming place nestled between rolling hills and flat meadows.

Photographs: left and below courtesy of Cainey Vineyard, by AV Photography; bottom left courtesy of Petros, by Cameron Ingalls

279

Gainey Vineyard
Character. Familiarity. Refreshing.

Boasting 150 acres of grapevines, rolling hills, and gracious oaks, Gainey Vineyard's appeal comes from a rich heritage and unrivaled distinctiveness that encourage guests to leave behind the busy notions of everyday life and step into a peaceful atmosphere and unbelievably gorgeous setting where every moment is important enough to savor.

Photographs: right by Sweet Monday; below by Baron Spafford Photography; bottom right by Evan Custon Photography

Nearly five decades ago, the Cainey family purchased 1,800 acres of land and developed it into the largest diversified farming operation in the Santa Ynez Valley. Vineyards became a successful part of the ranch as the family passionately took advantage of the unique geographical and climatic conditions: the warm, eastern end of the valley was conducive to growing Bordeaux varieties and the cool, western end suited pinot noir, chardonnay, and syrah. Central to every part of life was, and still is, the family's dedication to uncompromising quality that reflects the beauty and essence of the land.

Photographs by Andrew Van Cundy

With the same level of care and thoughtfulness that's lavished upon each lush fruit grown on the vines, weddings are embraced with undivided attention and contagious enthusiasm. Magnificent spaces support the serene ambience, whether mingling in the intimate. Spanish-style tasting room with its elk horn chandeliers, French antique furniture, and luxurious fireplace, lounging underneath sycamore trees in the spacious courtyard, or entertaining in one of the other equally inspiring spaces. At every turn, sweeping mountain and vineyard views imbue a desire simply to appreciate the present.

Photographs by Evan Guston Photography

Petros
Stimulating. Lofty. Commemorate.

Surrounded by 700 acres of vineyards, rambling oaks, and rolling hills, Petros is located within Fess Parker Wine Country Inn & Spa as a lovely venue for special occasions. The stunning setting combines elegant country atmosphere with upscale, authentic Hellenic cuisine, which native Greek restaurateur Petros Benekos has enhanced with a slight California touch. The light, airy space feels like a refreshing sigh, allowing the focus to remain on the celebration at hand.

Photographs: above and right courtesy of Petros; top right by Cameron Ingalls Photography

When it comes to catering...

Duo Catering & Events' owners Ashley Transki and Brian Congdon are simply brilliant. As with many local caterers, they focus on seasonal, local ingredients but somehow manage to create dishes that are simultaneously unbelievable and unpretentious. Village Modern Foods is another caterer that focuses on locally and seasonally based menus that are always creative; the team ensures a flawless event every time. I'm always hungry for delicious comfort food, so mouthwatering mac 'n cheese and juicy mini sliders are reason enough for me to love Pure Joy Catering, yet its creative presentation and plating takes the cuisine to an entirely new level. At New West, executive chef and owner Jeff Olsson bases his fare on seasonal, high-quality ingredients, creating the perfect blend of fine restaurant artistry with the versatility of catering. For something completely unique, Petros' Hellenic California cuisine is my choice; tantalizing taste and unrivaled quality is a guarantee. Chef Gabrielle Moes is in a class all her own at Seasons Catering, where she uses the nuances of spring, summer, winter, and fall to enliven every menu.

Photographs: left and bottom left courtesy of Duet Weddings, by Jose Villa; below courtesy of Petros, by Cameron Ingalls

Petros
Blend. Mouthwatering. Au courant.

Petros Benekos, a legend from his eponymous restaurants throughout California, has created something equally impressive with his catering, namely by carrying over the unique experience of perfectly blended Hellenic California cuisine from his restaurants into his catered dishes. Most companies only give one choice of salmon or steak, for example, offering guests little variety. Petros, however, creates an array of delectable dishes that are sure to make mouths water, smiles dance on guests' lips, and stomachs delightfully content. His creative freedom in the food choices for every event could even make it difficult to narrow down preferences for the actual menu; event planning by Alexandra Kolendrianos.

Photographs by Jose Villa

When it comes to floral design...

Camille Panzarello of Modern Day Design creates arrangements that perfectly model the wine country feeling: effortless, nonfussy, and natural with an unexpected finesse. I love watching Kate Holt of Flowerwild craft a design on the fly; Kate's loose, romantic designs translate into real elegance. No one could be more in tune with Santa Ynez Valley than Mindy Rice, who lives in the area, and it definitely shows. Renae's Bouquet is not just your run-of-the-mill florist either; using flowers imported from around the world, the modern innovative designs are always unique to each wedding.

Photographs: left and bottom left courtesy of Duet Weddings, by Jose Villa; below courtesy of Santa Ynez Inn, by Serena & Jason Photography

MRS. CLINT UNANDER

MR. CLINT UNANDER

When it comes to cakes and invitations...

The hands-on aspect is my favorite part. At Decadence Fine Cakes & Confections, where Dawn Peters makes everything from scratch, the cake-tasting session is to die for; not just one or two flavors, she breaks out her most creative confections to make sure you realize all of the options. It's no wonder that my mouth waters when I think of Enjoy Cupcakes, which bakes creative cakes and cupcakes in flavors like citrus sauvignon blanc and cherry vanilla merlot—perfect for wine country. Working with Jennifer Parsons at Tiny Pine Press is pretty high on my list of good times, too, especially when you see her at work on the letterpress machine at her studio. She is such an artist and has the unique ability to design stationery with real beauty and elegance without being overly formal. And creativity always permeates the air at Viola Sutanto's studio, Chewing the Cud, where every design is a true reflection of the couple.

Photographs: above left courtesy of Duet Weddings, by Jose Villa; above right and right courtesy of Cainey Vineyard, by AV Photography

Decadence Fine Cakes & Confections
Bliss. Savor. Sweet.

The sugary confections at Decadence are almost too pretty to eat—almost. One bite of a rich, sinfully tasty cake, cookie, cupcake, petit four, or other delicacy crafted by pastry chef and owner Dawn Peters will confirm that the unbelievably stunning creation was definitely made to eat and enjoy. Dawn even has those with special diet requirements covered; she makes these desserts as visually appealing and scrumptious as those traditionally prepared. With more than 15 years of professional experience, Dawn has developed relationships with numerous event planners, caterers, and florists, ensuring a smooth planning process and celebration.

Photographs: above by Elizabeth Messina Photography; top right by Todd Cicchi; right by This Modern Romance

When it comes to preserving memories...

In the Santa Ynez Valley, we are just bursting at the seams with talent. Born in the valley, Jose Villa only shoots in film; paired with his creative direction, his photos simply astound me and are truly timeless fine art pieces. Elizabeth Messina also favors film over digital and is known for innovatively capturing a magical, romantic ambience. From traveling the world over, Corbin Curkin has a special eye for taking just the right shot while letting the event unfold naturally. I am in awe of Max Wanger's incredible use of negative space; his images are breathtaking works of art. The region offers numerous highly talented videographers, but Joel Serrato Films, which I absolutely love, uses vintage cameras with super 8 mm and 16 mm film, which capture a depth and detail that just can't be achieved in any other manner.

Photographs: right and bottom right courtesy of Duet Weddings, by Jose Villa; below courtesy of Cainey Vineyard, by AV Photography

Destinations to Explore

From Beverly Hills, downtown LA, Malibu, and Orange County to Palm Springs, San Diego, Santa Barbara, Santa Monica, and the Santa Ynez Valley, Southern California certainly has no shortage of remarkable locales that, from everyone's perspective, would provide a spectacular spot for a wedding. Beyond those areas, the region has even more to offer brides, grooms, and their families and friends who are looking for that one special destination that will help them kick off the next joyful chapter in their lives.

From the Inland Empire, which includes the state's third-largest metropolitan area, to Ojai's community known for attracting artists, musicians, and health enthusiasts; from Pasadena—which means "crown of the valley" in Chippewa—to the stunning coastline of Manhattan Beach, residents and visitors alike will find unprecedented beauty, uniqueness, and romance. And even if you want to bring in the essence of a more distant setting, such as South Asian flair or the dreamy qualities of tropical island paradise, the amazing professionals in Southern California are more than capable of incorporating your every wish and desire.

Photographs: above ©iStockphoto.com/ekash; facing page ©iStockphoto.com/lightpix

South Asian Style on the West Coast

Many Southern California cities are cultural melting pots, and the weddings held there are no different. Nikki Khan's name is well known among Indian and Pakistani circles in the area: she's the undisputed South Asian wedding expert. Nikki coordinates more than just one big day, as South Asian weddings entail a host of attending festivities before and after the ceremony. Born in Pakistan, she gleaned the intricacies of social etiquette from a finishing school education in Switzerland, then broadened her horizons traveling the world and Europe for three years. She ended up in California for university; by 2001 she had turned her love of special events into her company Exquisite Events. South Asian weddings are Nikki's passion, and her background makes her well versed in the traditions, attire, cuisine, and languages involved. From the henna and sangeet to the ceremony and grand reception, Nikki coordinates, plans, and designs everything.

Photographs: right by Megan Stark Photography; below and bottom right by John Solano Photography

Exquisite Events by Nikki Khan
Vibrancy. Traditions. Culture.

Indian and Pakistani weddings unite more than two people: they bring two families together. These multi-day affairs encompass many social events that ensure guests mingle and spend time together, including joyous and colorful mehndi. During the fun-filled ritual, the bride receives intricate henna designs on her hands and feet. Escorted by her sisters and female cousins in a procession to the stage, the bride sits under a canopy amid decorated thaal platters of henna. During the henna process, Indian musicians accompany women clad in vivid colors, beautiful jewels, and embellished garments who circle the bride as they dance, sing, and engage in good-natured teasing of the couple's families.

Photographs: top left and right by Megan Stark Photography; above and left by Tara Arrowood Photography

293

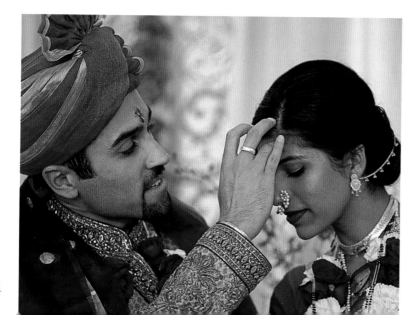

Sangeet is a colorful night full of fun, festivities, and drinking and dancing. As it takes place prior to the ceremony, during sangeet guests get acquainted with one another. Deep jewel tones pervade sangeet events, and the ballroom or private home's décor can go from that palette to cutting-edge. A joyous occasion marked by feasting, dancing, and singing, the sangeet is a vibrant party that kicks off the wedding revelry.

Photographs: top left, bottom left and above by Tara Arrowood Photography; middle left by Global Photography

The wedding ceremony is the centerpiece and crowning jewel of days of celebrations. The décor must be pitch-perfect and carefully situated to accommodate the fire at the heart of Hindu wedding rituals, considered a witness. Under the mandap structure that houses the ceremony, the bride and groom exchange garlands then conduct seven circuits around the fire. With each circuit, the couple makes a vow pertaining to some aspect of a happy relationship and household. After the ceremony, a meal is served before the bride and groom depart amid an emotional sendoff from family and guests.

Photographs: right by Tara Arrowood Photography; below and bottom right by Megan Stark Photography

Following the ceremony, the groom's parents may host a reception at their house. The full-scale reception including the bride and groom happens the next day, and it's an opportunity to shake off cultural traditions if desired and let loose with the Western-style clothing, customs, colors, and décor of the couple's choice.

Photographs by Daniel Boswell

As an event designer specializing in South Asian weddings, Nikki Khan plans every aspect of these celebrations, designing many separate parties in a range of styles. She's truly an expert at navigating the details of every day of the festivities, and it's no wonder she limits herself to about 20 celebrations a year.

Photographs: top left and right by Megan Stark Photography; above and right by John Solano Photography

Nikki's passion for coordinating special events extends beyond South Asian events and even beyond weddings and Southern California— she loves to design any sort of event, anywhere in the world. With Nikki, it's sure to be exquisite.

Photographs: above by Global Photography; right by John Solano Photography

Inland Empire

Encompassing a vast interior region of Southern California, including the cities of Riverside, San Bernardino, and Ontario, the Inland Empire is a historic center of agriculture home to citrus and dairy farms as well as vineyards and wineries that still produce substantial crops today. Businesses located here are distinguished by their ability to produce services matching the caliber of those closer to the sea at an unbelievably fantastic value.

Photographs courtesy of The Mission Inn Hotel & Spa

The Mission Inn Hotel & Spa
Timeless. Historic. Castle.

Surrounded by breathtaking architecture, timeless beauty, and Old World charm, The Mission Inn Hotel & Spa welcomes you to a destination where rich history, modern luxury, and classic elegance exist in perfect balance. As a National Historic Landmark, member of the Historic Hotels of America, and AAA four-diamond resort, The Mission Inn blends the romance and enchantment of a European castle with one-of-a-kind architecture masterminded by some of California's most famous architects. For over a century, world leaders and Hollywood stars—from Ronald and Nancy Reagan to screen legend Bette Davis—have married or honeymooned at The Mission Inn.

Photographs: right and bottom right by Cean One Photography; below and facing page courtesy of The Mission Inn Hotel & Spa

Encompassing 238 guestrooms and suites and 20,000 square feet of flexible function space, The Mission Inn offers dozens of overwhelmingly inspirational reception sites, including the region's only hotel chapel—the exquisite St. Francis of Assisi. Its majestic mahogany doors open to reveal the love of your life, warmly lit by the glow of Tiffany stained glass windows. Designed to perfectly serve all of your needs, from the rehearsal and ceremony to the reception and accommodations, the on-property staff of wedding professionals gracefully attend to every detail.

In addition to the magical atmosphere, The Mission Inn features a delightful array of award-winning amenities. Escape to Tuscan-inspired luxury at Kelly's Spa, as you toast to your new life together with poolside champagne, artful cuisine, and rejuvenating spa treatments. Experience AAA four-diamond dining and authentic flavors from around the world at the hotel's four restaurants and wine bar. Or relive history with a unique docent-led tour of the hotel from The Mission Inn Museum. Fill the first page of your new life together with treasured memories that transcend your wildest dreams and truly captivate all in attendance with a romantic setting that's almost as beautiful as how you feel inside.

Photographs: above and top by Cean One Photography; right courtesy of The Mission Inn Hotel & Spa

Manhattan Beach

Embodying a casual culture, Manhattan Beach is naturally the home of beach and indoor volleyball and a surfing hub that sees waves up to 12 feet high in the winter. The Pacific coastal town's breezy climate, excellent schools, low crime rate, and clean air make Manhattan Beach a much-desired place to live and visit. The city is a popular destination for seaside ceremonies and you're spoiled with choices when it comes to upscale places to repair to for the reception, rehearsal dinner, and any other wedding festivities.

Photographs: above and right courtesy of Shade Hotel, by Amy Theilig Photographic; top right courtesy of Petros, by Cameron Ingalls

Petros
Hellenic. Inventive. Dedicated.

Greece by way of California: Petros is a Manhattan Beach original. The Hellenic restaurant blends the authentic cuisine with the clean lines of white walls and cream linens. Founder Petros Benekos, raised in Athens and all across Europe and taught to cook by his mother and grandmother, prepares authentic dishes presented tastefully. The elegant space makes just the right setting for delectable dishes like feta-crusted lamb, Chilean sea bass, cucumber yogurt, and baklava. A variety of cheeses, coffee, and yogurt selections are several more traditional menu options that pay homage to Petros' birth country while giving patrons a taste of Greece in the middle of Manhattan Beach or, through catering, wherever your next celebration is located.

Photographs: right by Lapin Photography; below courtesy of Petros

Located in the post-modern Metlox Center mall, Petros is the place to find sophisticated locals and visitors chatting over Greek wine and contemporary music. Light and airy inside and out, the sprawling outdoor patio—complete with fountain in the middle of the courtyard—is perfect for enjoying the sunshine of a beautiful day or for gazing at the sunset. Simply put, the ambience and the cuisine are unbeatable.

Photographs: above courtesy of Petros; top right by Cary Moss Photography; right by Cameron Ingalls Photography

Shade Hotel
Upscale. Cool. Boutique.

Located two short blocks from the beach in perhaps the most picturesque seaside town in Southern California—Manhattan Beach—Shade Hotel guarantees a comfortable stay and dreamy venue for exquisite weddings. An open-air courtyard in the heart of the hotel is a much-coveted event spot. Award-winning executive chef Greg Hozinsky will whip up a tailor-made catering menu that will perfectly complement a one-of-a-kind wedding.

Photographs: top by Gabriel Ryan; above by Amy Theilig Photographic; right courtesy of Shade Hotel

Shade Hotel owner and restaurateur Michael Zislis has created his own personal paradise, complete with a rooftop dipping pool and the ultra-hip restaurant and lounge Zinc. Zinc serves breakfast, lunch, and small plates in the evening, and also features the longest bar in the South Bay. The penthouse suite includes a large bar area that possesses the same alluring ambience of Zinc and has its own beer tap and plasma TV. It's the ideal spot for the groom and his groomsmen to gather before the big day.

Photographs: right courtesy of Shade Hotel; below left and right by Brandon Humes, Couture Foto

There's even an exclusive bridal suite at Shade Hotel; it features a large bathroom, west side-facing balcony, dual powder areas, and lots of storage—everything necessary to prep for the wedding or unwind afterward. Couples who marry at the hotel enjoy a complimentary stay in a deluxe spa room the night of the ceremony. Among the luxurious amenities are Heat & Glo™ Cyclone fireplaces, Tempur-Pedic™ beds replete with Italian linens and the pillow of your choice, and chromatherapy settings that allow you to bathe the entire space in whatever color desired. Hidden behind a shoji screen is a two-person Sanijet™ bathtub also featuring chromatherapy lighting. Everyone who stays at the hotel enjoys in-room Lavazza espresso and coffee makers, the beach breakfast buffet, and complimentary use of beach cruiser bicycles—a requisite part of any Manhattan Beach sojourn.

Photographs: above courtesy of Shade Hotel; top right by Hill Street Studios; right by Amy Theilig Photographic

Ojai

Ojai is a picturesque city situated inside the Ojai Valley at the foot of hills and mountains. Numerous films have amply showcased its beauty, and many celebrities have been drawn to make homes within its limits. Every year Ojai plays host to a film festival, music festival, wine festival, and playwrights' conference, and boasts gorgeous natural resources from Los Padres National Forest to Matilija Creek to Lake Casitas. Golf is big in Ojai too, with two major courses adding a touch of perfectly manicured order to the existing charm.

Photographs courtesy of Ojai Valley Inn & Spa: above by Amy & Stuart Photography: right by A Bryan Photo

Ojai Valley Inn & Spa
Dramatic. Spanish. Vistas.

Nestled in the lush Ojai Valley amid lavender fields and tranquil courtyards, Ojai Valley Inn & Spa is truly a refuge. The Spanish Colonial Revival architecture found throughout Ojai pervades the resort, and the majestic mountains surrounding the town form the perfect backdrop for gorgeous weddings. Sunset ceremonies are particularly stunning, as Ojai—one of the few places in the world with an east-west mountain range—has a "pink moment" when the fading sunlight casts a brilliant shade of pink over the east end of the valley. Whether staying at the resort for lodging or event purposes, the world-class amenities and beautiful scenery make it easy to unwind.

Ojai Valley Inn and the town of Ojai share a storied history woven inextricably together. Much of Ojai was masterminded by entrepreneur Edward D. Libbey, and the resort is no exception: as early as 1923, he dreamed of a golf course and country club that would harmonize with the rural, undeveloped landscape. By 1930 guestrooms had been added to his secluded oasis—built in the Spanish style consistent with the town— and guests soon described it as a hidden getaway. In 2005 the resort received an extensive renovation at no cost to the original charm and sense of place.

Photographs: this page courtesy of Ojai Valley Inn & Spa; facing page by Jose Villa

Weddings are where the Ojai Valley Inn & Spa really shines: the setting is intimate, the view is breathtaking, the service is impeccable, and the food is delectable. No matter the style—country, rustic, formal, chic—the resort will set the stage. An array of beautiful ceremony sites is matched only by the diversity of the reception possibilities—indoors and out. Ceremonies, receptions, and all the attending festivities are customized to suit the couple's tastes, and in the meantime, guests will enjoy making the most of all the resort has to offer in the way of leisure. The Ojai Valley Inn & Spa hosts unforgettable weddings for couples and guests alike.

Photographs: left by A Bryan Photo; below by Amy & Stuart Photography; facing page by Stephanie Hogue Photography

Ojai Valley Inn & Spa is a sophisticated escape that feels like a private country estate. The five-diamond quality amenities include luxurious Spanish Colonial rooms, five dining options, four pools, bicycle rentals, activities for children and teens, numerous fitness classes, four tennis courts, a spa, a championship golf course, and a three-acre herb garden for strolling, dining, or reflecting. Wedding parties at the resort can relax indoors or out. Spa Ojai, perfect for pre-wedding spa parties, encompasses a veritable village of calm and rejuvenation. You'll discover everything from signature treatments to an apothecary to learn how to blend essential oils into custom-made lotions to give as favors or gifts.

Pasadena

Most famous for hosting the annual Rose Bowl football game and Tournament of Roses parade, Pasadena is home to many scientific and cultural institutions. A jewel in the San Gabriel Valley, Pasadena is bounded by the San Rafael Hills and the San Gabriel Mountains. Wherever you go in Pasadena, gorgeous towering mountain views surround you; the relaxed, calm vibe of the city can largely be accredited to its geography. Richly steeped in culture and education, Pasadena makes an elegant choice for hosting festivities.

Photographs courtesy of The Langham Huntington, left by Jan Carcia Photography, bottom left by Victor Sizemore Photography; below courtesy of The Langham Huntington

The Langham Huntington, Pasadena
Captivating. Indulgence. Getaway.

For a wedding imbued with classic romance, look no further than The Langham Huntington, Pasadena. With the picturesque San Gabriel Mountains as a backdrop and located minutes from downtown Los Angeles, this elegant hotel is the perfect blend of urban and idyllic.

The Langham's 23 acres encompass meticulous gardens and grand ballrooms, as well as 380 guestrooms, suites, and cottages. Open since 1907 and channeling the luxury and hospitality of London's original Langham—Europe's first grand hotel—The Langham is a Pasadena landmark combining luxury with serenity. Four dining choices, an outdoor pool heated year-round, a spa, fitness center, three tennis courts, bicycle rentals, nearby golf course, and many activities round out the spectacular benefits to hosting and staying at The Langham.

Photographs: left by Victor Sizemore; below courtesy of The Langham Huntington; bottom left by Louis Felix

The hotel's lush grounds are perfect for outdoor wedding ceremonies followed by elegant ballroom receptions. From an exotic Japanese garden with serene landscaping and striking red bridge to a stately sloping garden that comes with the rare chance to enter via horse-drawn carriage, vintage car, or even a small elephant, the outdoor venues are second to none. Follow the tranquility with opulent romance in one of three historic ballrooms. The indoor spaces have glamour and grandeur in spades, along with an array of antique accoutrements. Banquet rooms for smaller indoor ceremonies and receptions are another option The Langham provides. The menus and décor will be tailor-made by a team of experts to fit each couple's tastes and style.

Photographs: above and top left and facing page courtesy of The Langham Huntington; left by Duke Photography

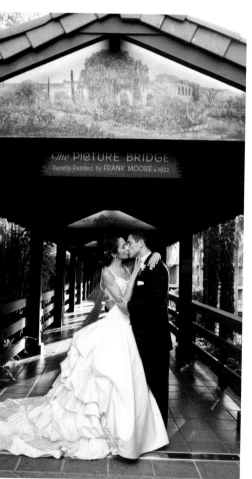

No wedding at The Langham is complete without a visit to its renowned Huntington Spa, a destination in and of itself. With 11,000 square feet, it's a true haven of sublime indulgence. Massages, facials, and body treatments take place in 13 rooms, including a couple's room for the bride and groom to bask in a joint massage before or after the big day. The full-service salon offers manicures, pedicures, and make-up and hair services. The spa is unique in that it also provides treatments based on traditional Chinese medicine techniques. Acupuncture, cupping, moxibustion, and ear seeds are several of the available options not seen on every spa menu. These services unite the five elements and promote overall wellness.

Photographs: top and above by Jan Carcia, left by Duke Photography

The Langham is delighted to assist with every wedding detail, from cuisine to linens to lodging to music. Professional wedding coordinators partner with The Langham staff to manage all components and formulate a schedule to ensure everything goes off without a hitch thanks to behind-the-scenes planning. Enjoy gorgeous wedding portraits against breathtaking mountain vistas, chef-designed cuisine, lush and refined event spaces, calming accommodations and beauty treatments, and attentive service all in one place at Pasadena's grand luxury hotel.

Photographs: right by Desi Bayton; below by Karen French; bottom right courtesy of The Langham Huntington

Inspiration from the Tropics

Nothing reminds you of a cherished island sojourn more vividly than a beautiful floral design, whether it's full of fabulously exotic shapes and textures, bursting with vibrant colors, or simply has an aroma so sweet the arrangement seems almost edible. Considering Southern California's temperate climate and stunning ocean views, the region provides the perfect backdrop to conjure up images of idyllic isles. This multisensory experience—so evocative of life in the tropics, reminiscent of island honeymoons—is precisely what inspires Mille Fiori Floral Design to bring its unique brand of creativity to special events of all sorts—whether a simple pre-nuptial brunch, an oceanside ceremony, an elaborate post-wedding celebration, or any other occasion that calls for the perfect floral motifs.

Photographs by Marianne Lozano

Mille Fiori Floral Design
Vessels. Flowers. Fabulous.

While many floral studios thrive exclusively on the concept of creating visually beautiful arrangements, Cina Park's Mille Fiori Floral Design isn't content until the design is not only pretty but also clever, fresh, and timeless in style. Cina and her team love coming up with truly innovative ways to present their flowers. Whether sprouting from a traditional vase, dangling from the ceiling, pavéd to an unusual vessel, floating in a swimming pool, submerged in a glass cylinder, sprinkled loosely amidst a collection of family heirlooms, displayed in a shadow box, or otherwise showcased, the floral creations of Mille Fiori are nothing short of breathtaking.

Photographs by 2me Photography

Mille Fiori's designers insist that the concept need not be overly complex in order to be successful. A single type or color of flower used in mass quantity would yield a very different effect than an arrangement that utilized dozens of different types of flowers in varying hues, but both options have the potential to dazzle the eyes and senses—it's all in the execution. And knowing precisely how to create the right look for the occasion is what Gina and her team do best.

Photographs by 2me Photography

Southern California WEDDINGS

SOUTHERN CALIFORNIA TEAM

PUBLISHER: Brian G. Carabet

PUBLISHER: John A. Shand

VICE PRESIDENT & SENIOR PUBLISHER: Carla Bowers

SENIOR GRAPHIC DESIGNER: Emily A. Kattan

GRAPHIC DESIGNER: Lilian Oliveira

GRAPHIC DESIGNER: Paul Strength

MANAGING EDITOR: Rosalie Z. Wilson

EDITOR: Alicia Berger

EDITOR: Anita Kasmar

EDITOR: Jennifer Nelson

EDITOR: Sarah Tangney

EDITOR: Lindsey Wilson

MANAGING PRODUCTION COORDINATOR: Kristy Randall

PRODUCTION COORDINATOR: London Nielsen

PROJECT COORDINATOR: Laura Greenwood

TRAFFIC SUPERVISOR: Drea Williams

ADMINISTRATIVE COORDINATOR: Amanda Mathers

CLIENT SUPPORT COORDINATOR: Kelly Traina

ADMINISTRATIVE ASSISTANT: Tommie Runner

PANACHE PARTNERS, LLC
CORPORATE HEADQUARTERS
1424 Cables Court
Plano, TX 75075
469.246.6060
www.panache.com

RESOURCES

CAKE DESIGN

The Butter End Cakery
www.thebutterend.com

CAKE
www.fabcakes.com

Charm City Cakes
www.charmcitycakeswest.com

Christine Dahl Pastries
www.santabarbaracakes.com

Decadence Fine Cakes
& Confections 288
Dawn Peters
201 Industrial Way, Suite C
Buellton, CA 93427
805.686.2860
www.decadenceweddingcakes.com

Enjoy Cupcakes
www.enjoycupcakes.com

Fantasy Frostings 171
Leslie Maynor-Anderson
301 Pasadena Avenue
South Pasadena, CA 91030
626.799.2900
www.fantasyfrostings.com

Filigree Cakes 141
Sunny Lee
Irvine, CA
888.335.2253
www.filigreecakes.com

Hansen's Cakes
www.hansencakes.com

Heslington Cakes, LLC. 142
Sara Heslington
PO Box 397
Corona del Mar, CA 92625
949.478.5207
www.heslingtoncakes.com

Joanie & Leigh's Cake Divas. 42
Leigh Grode
Joan Spitler
241 ½ South Beverly Drive, Suite 1
Beverly Hills, CA 90212
310.248.CAKE(2253)
www.cakedivas.com

Let Them Eat Cake
www.letthemeatcake.net

Michele Coulon Dessertier
www.dessertier.com

Rosebud Cakes
www.rosebudcakes.com

Sweet and Saucy Shop
www.sweetandsaucyshop.com

Sweet Cheeks Baking Co. 192
Elaine Ardizzone
4564 Alvarado Cyn Road, Suite A
San Diego, CA 92120
619.285.1220
www.sweetcheeksbaking.com

Sweet Lady Jane
www.sweetladyjane.com

Vanilla Bake Shop. 259
512 Wilshire Boulevard
Santa Monica, CA 90401
310.458.6644
www.vanillabakeshop.com

CATERING

24 Carrots
www.24carrots.com

An Catering. 30, 131, 163, 251
Catherine An
2700 Colorado Avenue, Suite 190
Santa Monica, CA 90404
323.460.2645
www.ancatering.com

Coast Catering by Barry Layne 186
Barry Layne
Jennifer Layne
San Diego, CA
877.577.1718
www.coastcatering.com

Crème de la Crème
Gourmet Foods and Catering
www.cremedelacremefoods.com

Crown Point Catering
www.crownpointcatering.com

Dining Details
www.diningdetails.com

Duo Catering & Events 217
Ashley Transki
Brian Congdon
614 E. Haley Street
Santa Barbara, CA 93103
805.957.1670
www.duoevents.com

The Food Matters
www.thefoodmatters.com

Giuseppe Restaurants & Fine Catering
www.giuseppecatering.com

Good Gracious
www.goodgraciousevents.com

Hasmik Party Services
www.hasmikparty.com

Heirloom LA
www.heirloomla.com

Jackson Somerset
www.alanjacksoncatering.com

Jay's Catering
www.jayscatering.com

Joan's on Third 93
Carol McNamara
8350 West 3rd Street
Los Angeles, CA 90048
323.655.2285
www.joansonthird.com

The Kitchen for Exploring Foods 31
Peggy Dark
1434 West Colorado Boulevard
Pasadena, CA 91105
626.793.7218
www.thekitchen.net

Miranda's Catering
www.mirandascatering.com

New West Catering
www.newwestcatering.com

Patina Restaurant Group
www.patinagroup.com

INVITATION DESIGN

LIGHTING & EVENT DESIGN

Ambient Event Design...................232
Geoff Mognis
PO Box 21232
Santa Barbara, CA 93121
805.886.8444
www.ambientevent.com

Bella Vista Designs......................233
Trevor Zellet
1 North Calle Cesar Chavez, Suite 9
Santa Barbara, CA 93103
805.966.9616
www.bellavistadesigns.com

Concepts Event Design..................196
Haydee and Federico Alderete
436 West 8th Street, Suite D
National City, CA 91950
619.336.0202
www.conceptseventdesign.com

Lighten Up, Inc 148, 261
Nathan Megaw
8341 Hindry Avenue
Los Angeles, CA 90045
Los Angeles: 310.670.8515
Orange County: 949.566.9878
www.lightenupinc.com

MAKEUP & HAIR DESIGN

Beauty by Berit 147
Berit Digerud
949.444.1474
Laguna Beach, CA
www.BeautyByBerit.com

Tiffany Monday—Exquisite Beauty.......198
Orange County: 949.697.5440
San Diego: 858.215.1161
www.tiffanymonday.com

PHOTOGRAPHY

Aaron Delesie
www.delesieblog.com

Amy & Stuart Photography
www.amyandstuart.com

Barnett Photographics
www.barnettphoto.com

BB Photography 229
Brian Charrette
Brady Charrette
241 Las Ondas
Santa Barbara, CA 93109
805.682.9358
www.bb-photo.com

Boyd Harris Photographs
www.boydharris.com

Corbin Gurkin
www.corbingurkin.com

Elizabeth Messina Photography.........103
Elizabeth Messina
Los Angeles, CA
310.779.9151
www.kissthegroom.com
www.elizabethmessina.com

Jasmine Star
www.jasmine-star.com

Jay Lawrence Goldman
Photography......................... 48, 105
Jay Lawrence Goldman
6139 Wilshire Boulevard
Los Angeles, CA 90048
323.954.7436
www.jlgweddings.com

Jessica Claire
www.jessicaclaire.net

Joe Buissink
www.joebuissink.com

John & Joseph Photography Inc 144
John Hong
Joseph Hong
1800 Berkeley Street, Suite B
Santa Monica, CA 90404
310.883.5803
www.johnandjoseph.com

John Russo Photography..................49
John Russo
9663 Santa Monica Boulevard, Suite 626
Beverly Hills, CA 90210
323.653.7774
www.johnrussoweddings.com

John Solano Photography................ 50
John Solano
Beverly Hills, CA 90212
310.205.0976
www.imagemakr.com

Jose Villa
www.josevillaphoto.com

Joy Marie Photography
www.joymariephoto.com

Luna Photo
www.lunaphoto.com

Max Wanger
www.maxwanger.com

Melissa Musgrove Photography........230
Melissa Musgrove
2821 Serena Road
Santa Barbara, CA 93105
805.563.5050
www.melissamusgrove.com

Miki & Sonja Photography
www.mikiandsonja.com

Paul Barnett
www.barnettphoto.com

Samuel Lippke Studios...................145
Samuel Lippke
4720 East 2nd Street, No. 5
Long Beach, CA 90803
562.343.2676
www.samuellippke.com

Simone & Martin Photography
www.simonemartin.com

Stephanie Hogue Photography........ 231
Stephanie Hogue
Ventura, CA
805.642.5257
www.hoguephoto.com

Tim Otto Photography....................195
Tim Otto
4901 Morena Boulevard, Suite 209A
San Diego, CA 92117
858.273.5889
www.timotto.com

True Photography Weddings
www.truephotographyweddings.com

Victor Sizemore
www.vcsphoto.com

Yitzhak Dalal Photography................51
Yitzhak Dalal
3328 Oak Glen Drive
Los Angeles, CA 90068
323.654.6465
www.dalalphotography.com

Yvette Roman Photography
www.yrphoto.com

RENTALS

Roberta Karsch
6900 Canby Avenue, Suite 106
Reseda, CA 91335
818.343.3451
www.resourceoneinc.com

Richard LoGuercio
7725 Airport Business Park Way
Van Nuys, CA 91406
818.908.4211
www.tacer.biz

RESTAURANTS

Madelina Silva
21150 Pacific Coast Highway
Malibu, CA 90265
310.317.6204
www.dukesmalibu.com

NOBU
903 North La Cienega Boulevard
Los Angeles, CA 90069
310.657.5711
www.noburestaurants.com

Tina Takaya
Richard Yates
1325 State Street
Santa Barbara, CA 93101
805.966.9676
www.opalrestaurantandbar.com

1316 State Street
Santa Barbara, CA 91301
805.899.9100
www.petrosrestaurant.com

VENUES

Annenberg Community Beach House
beachhouse.smgov.net

Bel-Air Bay Club
www.belairbayclub.com

Robert Church Haggstrom
Karen Waldron
6415 Busch Drive
Malibu, CA 90265
310.457.0600
www.churchestatevineyards.com

Cicada
www.cicadarestaurant.com

Culy Warehouse
www.culywarehouse.com

Demetria Estate
www.demetriaestate.com

Estate Weddings and Events
www.estateweddingsandevents.com

Figueroa Mountain Farmhouse
www.figueroamountainfarmhouse.com

Dan H. Gainey
3950 East Highway 246
Santa Ynez, CA 93460
805.688.0558
www.gaineyvineyard.com

Gull's Way
By appointment only,
contact Mindy Weiss

Lotusland
www.lotusland.org

Marvimon
www.marvimon.com

Montecito Country Club
www.montecitocc.com

Museum of Contemporary Art
www.mcasandiego.org

Old Mission Santa Barbara
www.santabarbaramission.org

Petros Benekos
451 Manhattan Beach Boulevard
Manhattan Beach, CA 90266
310.545.4100
www.petrosrestaurant.com

Rancho Las Lomas
www.rancholaslomas.com

The Richard Nixon Presidential Library
www.specialevents.nixonfoundation.org

Rocky Oaks Estate
www.rockyoaksestate.com

Saddle Rock Ranch
www.malibufamilywines.com

The San Diego Museum of Art
www.sdmart.org

Ariana Nobel
Ellen Reid
3300 Via Real
Carpinteria, CA 93013
805.684.6683
www.sbpolo.com

Scripps Seaside Forum
www.sio.ucsd.edu

Dora Wexell
891 Laguna Canyon Road
Laguna Beach, CA 92651
949.376.1555
www.seven-degrees.com

Tiato—Kitchen Bar Garden Venue
Catherine An
2700 Colorado Avenue, Suite 190
Santa Monica, CA 90404
323.460.2645
www.tiato.com

Vibiana
www.vibianala.com

Zaca Creek Ranch
www.zacacreekranch.com

VIDEOGRAPHY

David Robin Films
www.davidrobinfilms.com

Joel Serrato Films
www.joelserratofilms.com

Living Cinema
www.livingcinema.net

Paper Tape Films
www.papertapefilms.com

Reel Life Pictures
www.reelifepictures.com

Vidicam Productions
www.vidicamproductions.com

THE PANACHE COLLECTION

Dream Homes Series

An Exclusive Showcase of the
Finest Architects, Designers and Builders

Carolinas
Chicago
Coastal California
Colorado
Deserts
Florida
Georgia
Los Angeles
Metro New York
Michigan
Minnesota
New England

New Jersey
Northern California
Ohio & Pennsylvania
Pacific Northwest
Philadelphia
South Florida
Southwest
Tennessee
Texas
Washington, D.C.

Spectacular Homes Series

An Exclusive Showcase of the Finest Interior Designers

California
Carolinas
Chicago
Colorado
Florida
Georgia
Heartland
London
Michigan
Minnesota
New England

Metro New York
Ohio & Pennsylvania
Pacific Northwest
Philadelphia
South Florida
Southwest
Tennessee
Texas
Toronto
Washington, D.C.
Western Canada

Perspectives on Design Series

Design Philosophies Expressed
by Leading Professionals

California
Carolinas
Chicago
Colorado
Florida
Georgia
Great Lakes
London

Minnesota
New England
New York
Pacific Northwest
South Florida
Southwest
Toronto
Western Canada

Art of Celebration Series

Inspiration and Ideas from
Top Event Professionals

Chicago & the Greater Midwest
Colorado
Georgia
New England
New York
Northern California
South Florida
Southern California
Southern Style
Southwest
Toronto
Washington, D.C.

City by Design Series

An Architectural Perspective

Atlanta
Charlotte
Chicago
Dallas
Denver
New York
Orlando
Phoenix
San Francisco
Texas

Spectacular Wineries Series

A Captivating Tour of Established,
Estate and Boutique Wineries

California's Central Coast
Napa Valley
New York
Ontario
Sonoma County
Texas
Washington

Experience Series

The Most Interesting Attractions,
Hotels, Restaurants, and Shops

Austin & Hill Country
Boston
British Columbia
Chicago
Southern California
Twin Cities

Interiors Series

Leading Designers Reveal Their Most Brilliant Spaces

Florida
Midwest
New York
Southeast
Washington, D.C.

Spectacular Golf Series

An Exclusive Collection of Great Golf Holes

Arizona
Colorado
Florida
Georgia
Ontario
Pacific Northwest
Texas
Western Canada

Weddings

Captivating Destinations and Exceptional Resources
Introduced by the Finest Event Planners

Southern California Weddings

Specialty Titles

The Finest in Unique Luxury Lifestyle Publications

21st Century Homes
Cloth and Culture: Couture Creations of Ruth E. Funk
Distinguished Inns of North America
Extraordinary Homes California
Geoffrey Bradfield Ex Arte
Into the Earth: A Wine Cave Renaissance
Luxurious Interiors
Napa Valley Iconic Wineries
Shades of Green Tennessee
Spectacular Hotels
Spectacular Restaurants of Texas
Visions of Design

Panache Books App

Inspiration at Your Fingertips

Download the Panache Books
app in the iTunes Store to
access the digital version of
Southern California Weddings
and other Panache Partners
publications. Each book offers
inspiration at your fingertips.

Panache Partners, LLC   1424 Gables Court   Plano, Texas 75075   469.246.6060   www.panache.com